"Try to Survive

...and Tell the World"

Fulfillment of a Promise

Personal Recollections

of a Holocaust Survivor

Who escaped from Auschwitz

Rose Ickowicz Rechnic

The words written in this memoir are all true as remembered by the author.

To arrange for speaking engagements or to obtain copies of *Try to Survive,* please contact:

Rose Rechnic
E-mail: roserechnic@aol.com

ISBN 0-615-12056-3

Library of Congress Cataloging-in-Publication Data

A portion of the proceeds from the sale of *Try to Survive* will be donated to organizations and institutions dedicated to preserving the memory of the Holocaust.

Cover design by: Rose I. Rechnic
                          Janis Galitzeck
                          Paul Evans

Published in the U.S.A. by REAL PRESS, 2002

Printed in the U.S.A. by Alcom Printing, 2002

DEDICATION

*This book is dedicated in loving
memory of my family
who perished in the Holocaust.*

For my dear children
Elaine and Alice,
And my grandchildren
Marci, Hayley, Wendy,
Stephanie and Marc,
Who warm my heart and soul.

TABLE OF CONTENTS

Acknowledgements

I've always wanted to write my memoirs but I never got around to it until now, pretty late in life.

In July 2001, Gail Rosenthal, director of the Holocaust Resource Center at the Richard Stockton College of New Jersey, asked me to address a Holocaust and Genocide Education class of prospective teachers. I had recently moved to Atlantic City from Hallandale, Florida, and I was happy to accept this invitation and continue with what I have been doing for so many years. It would add a dimension to my new life in New Jersey.

At the end of my presentation, during the question/answer period, I was asked, "Why didn't you write a memoir?"

"I wanted to," I answered, "but I didn't think I was quite capable of this task and, moreover, I was always distracted by my busy life.

But Gail Rosenthal and Maryann McLoughlin insisted: "We'll help you!"

I came home full of enthusiasm, pulled out a notebook and started writing. Everyday I wrote a few pages and was amazed at how vivid were my recollections of my life experiences. If I were not sure of an event or details, I would discuss them for hours with my friend Esther Peterseil, who was in Auschwitz at the same time as I was. She helped confirm some events and names for which I am grateful. My girlfriend Marysia helped me to recall the story pertaining to the jewelry in Bergen-Belsen. I did not remember it, but I was happy to include the story, for it helped save her life and showed my decency under horrible circumstances. Marysia Rodin is my very dear friend and a wonderful human being.

But, first and foremost, my gratitude goes to Dr. McLoughlin, whose guidance, encouragement, kindness, and devotion to this project have been priceless. She was always there for me. Without her, this memoir would not have been accomplished. She typed and edited the first draft of my manuscript from its initial handwritten state, a task that took a great deal of time and patience and for which I am very grateful. Thanks, also, to Jan Jenkins for her assistance in typing.

I want to express my gratitude to my children and grandchildren for their daily encouragement and their expressions of pride in me. The feeling is mutual; I am very proud of them. Their tender loving care of my husband and me—they have almost become our parents—is so touching.

I also want to thank my children and grandchildren for their feedback and suggestions during the writing of this book. Their input was invaluable. My deepest gratitude goes to my daughter, Alice, who spent countless hours with me editing the final manuscript and taking care of technical issues connected with the publishing of this book. She tells me it was a labor of love.

Last, but not least, I thank my dear husband for being at my side now and for fifty-six years. I am very fortunate!

INTRODUCTION

Second Generation

By daughters

Elaine and Alice

The term Holocaust, from a historical perspective, is relatively new, but has become a part of the collective vernacular designating the unprecedented period in history depicted in our mother's book. Our mother is a Survivor. Our father is a Survivor. My sister and I, and all Survivors' children are known as Second Generation.

Survivor. We capitalize it, because it demands a proper name. It refers to those individuals who walked out of the ashes of the Holocaust—a unique group for which there is no comparable experience.

It took 50 years, but the world was finally ready and eager to hear, to read, and to discuss this darkest of periods in history. In the last decade there has been much written and documented in newspapers, books, films, and museums describing every historical detail, relating countless stories of horror and recovery. It is virtually impossible to absorb the magnitude of human suffering endured. Every Survivor's story stands alone and each depicts the resilience of the human spirit in defiance of man's horrific inhumanity to man. Our mother's book is one unforgettable story.

We don't remember ever *not* knowing about the Holocaust. From our first conscious memories as children, my sister and I knew. We remember asking questions, the same ones and new ones, over and over again. Our mother never denied us answers. In fact, she never denied anyone answers. All you had to do was ask. She gave answers with measured appropriateness and often, unbelievably, with humor to children and adults alike. The Holocaust wasn't just a part of our lives; it was woven into the very fabric of our lives, and shaped every aspect of our existence.

We were different. Our parents had accents; our mother had large numbers tattooed on her arm. We had no grandparents and little extended family. There were no family albums of generations that came before and no family heirlooms passed on to future generations. There was loneliness on holidays and sadness in our parent's painful memories. The Holocaust was our history. We knew about it, but surprisingly, many American Jews and non-Jews alike did not. Many did not want to know, but for those who were interested, our mother informed, educated, and enlightened. It was her mission, her duty to fulfill her mother's final plea to "try to survive and tell the world" so they would know and never forget. She has honored her mother's wish. This book is the culmination of that pledge.

Our mother is blessed with an enduring, exceptional memory, which, at the age of 76, far surpasses ours and continues to astound us. She is also blessed with the gift of language, with the ability to weave words together beautifully on paper, in poetry, and in song, always on key. In her book she strikes the perfect note, conveying the unspeakable, while engaging her listeners and readers with vivid images, both haunting and uplifting.

There has been so much written about the Holocaust. So how and why is this book different? Because the style and spirit in which it was written embodies our mother's unique essence. Her book reads so naturally, so innocently, so truthfully, so ingenuously. And those qualities epitomize our mother. Without pretense, it tells a story that is painful to read, yet impossible to put down.

We've heard most of the story before but there are new revelations. We've grown up knowing, yet we still cannot imagine that she survived and that our father survived. How? How could anyone survive? And beyond survival, how could anyone live a happy, productive life? Our parents have done just that. They defied Hitler. We are in awe of them, and as our legacy as Second Generation, we protect them. They have suffered enough. We want them never again to experience pain in their lives.

Our mother's perfectly wonderful childhood was cut short at the age of 13 when the Nazi horror struck and destroyed the tranquility of her life. We often reflect upon her nature and her personality and conclude that, emotionally in many ways, she still seems to be a young adolescent filled with wonder, curiosity, and a thirst for knowledge that, to this day, is insatiable.

While our father was more mature, serious, and cautious, our mother was more like a peer in many ways. We grew up with her, in a sense. Our childhood experiences were her vicarious adventures. It was as if she had to fill a huge gap to make up for precious lost years, opportunities, and relationships, of which she was so brutally, robbed. Our friends loved being with her because she was so fanciful and open and fun. She was "one of the girls" whenever she joined in on our conversations. We would stay up through the night watching old movies with her. She became a typical stage mother savoring every rehearsal and performance. How she loved the whole make-believe world of movies and theater. Entertainment and an escape— one and the same. Our mother, our friend.

And yet, she is a paradox: so innocent and naïve, yet fatalistic and courageous; strong willed and determined, yet easily hurt and disappointed; thick skinned to outsiders, yet vulnerable to those who truly know her; fun-loving, yet profound; social, yet lonely; outspoken, yet achingly silent. She is loving, devoted, vibrant, vital, creative, intelligent, and always interesting.

Our mother has accomplished so much. Nothing she touches is ordinary. Everything she does is with style, from fashion to decorating to the smallest gesture. Our homes and wardrobes have always reflected her talent for design and her eye for detail, which she carries into every project and undertaking. She consistently seeks new challenges and, in turn, challenges others.

We used to speculate as to what she might have achieved in life had the war not intervened. Nevertheless, our mother's resume is quite remarkable. She has worn many hats (literally and figuratively!), carried many professional business cards, and touched many lives beyond those of her children and grandchildren. She continues to educate and interact with high school and college students who express to her their overwhelming admiration and respect upon hearing her story.

Our mother has given our family a legacy for which we will forever be grateful and promise to perpetuate. We are very proud of our extraordinary mother. Thank you, our dearest Mommy, for your gift of love and for writing this book for our children, future generations and us who live because you survived.

Third Generation

By grandchildren

Marci, Hayley, Wendy, Stephanie, and Marc

Our grandparents are Holocaust survivors. We have known this for as long as we can remember. It is not simply a fact about our grandparents' past. Rather, it is a defining factor in all of our lives. We speak as one, expressing our collective thoughts and feelings.

When we think about what our grandparents have experienced, we grieve for the years of their lives that were lost and for family members we will never know. At the same time, we are overwhelmed by gratitude for our good fortune to know, love, and learn from our grandparents first hand. We are eternally cognizant of the preciousness of their love and presence in our lives. Because our mothers never knew their grandparents, we never take for granted sharing our everyday experiences, holidays, and milestones with them.

We look at our grandparents and want to protect and nurture them, to save them from pain after the hardship they have already endured. Yet in them we see an incomprehensible strength, which we can only hope to have inherited and pray never to need, that allowed them to overcome the atrocities of the Holocaust and create a new life in the wake of so much destruction.

Our grandmother, in particular, has always been vocal in sharing her experience with our family and with others, Jews and non-Jews of all ages and races. She has been a leader, educating generation after generation through lectures, audio and video testimonials, and other speaking engagements over many years. This book, documenting her story as a teaching tool, continues in the tradition of her lifelong commitment to ensuring that the world does not forget about the millions of Jews whose lives were sacrificed to anti-Semitism.

Our grandmother's persistence in telling her story—from behind the podium, on tape, and now in the written word—is ever more admirable in the framework of her multi-faceted life which continues to unfold.

While our grandmother is a vocal and visible survivor, she is much more than that. She is accomplished as a wife, a mother, a grandmother, a friend, a teacher, an entrepreneur, a decorator, an interpreter, a poet, an author, an activist, an organizational leader and event planner, and an evolving woman with more achievements to come. Her vibrant life embodies the defeat of the Nazis. She has not only survived, but she has thrived.

This is our legacy. We will always be the descendants of survivors, representing our grandparents' triumph. We will always tell their story. And our children and grandchildren will become messengers and symbols of survival as well.

While we have inherited the responsibility of sharing our grandparents' stories as our birthright, we ask that all who know them adopt this mission as well. If you are touched by this memoir, if her story expands your perspective, strengthens your resolve against anti-Semitism or reminds you of a history too often pushed to the back of your mind, please pass on our grandmother's words.

Our admiration for our grandmother is endless. She has lived her life with love and purpose so that six million other Jews will not have died in vain. We are grateful for the gifts she has passed on to her family—her love, her wit, her intellect, and her story. In all our lives, we will use the tools she has given us and will use them well, following our grandmother's shining example.

Mem'ry

Music from *Cats*
Lyrics by Rose Rechnic

Mem'ry, of a town in Zaglembie
Of our mothers and fathers
And a life that was sweet . . .
I remember that town and Jewish culture that thrived
Now just the Mem'ry is alive.
Mem'ry, of the pain and the sorrow
With no hope for tomorrow
Or the future ahead . . .
We survived without knowing what the next day
would bring,
Still today, we're remembering.
Remember when we lived in fear
With pain and death all around.
We survived against impossible odds,
Now, the tragic past is behind us.
Stand tall, we're survivors that wouldn't fall,
We will always remember,
We must never forget.
Our dear ones who perished "Al Hakidush Haschem"
With all our love, we remember them . . .
Stand tall, we're the chosen that didn't fall
We gave birth to a new "Dor"*
For us to carry on.
We're survivors
With children who have learned from our past
Keep the mem'ry, let it last!!!!!!!!!

*"Generation".

Chapter 1

END OF PARADISE

It was late August 1939 in the countryside resort in the Beskid Mountains of Poland. We were saying goodbye to the people who spent the summer with us in the villa—two other families with children, and four female students from Warsaw. We had spent the entire summer in the mountains, as we did every year.

Our mother Andzia, my sister Bronia, fifteen years old, my little eight-year-old brother Marek and I, thirteen at the time, escaped to the countryside to enjoy the fresh air and be fed five times daily in order to gain weight—chubby meant prosperous! My father, Abel, who was an accountant in a large iron company, joined us every weekend. He never actually took a summer vacation; instead he chose to work in order to double his summer salary.

The two-story villa my parents rented that summer of 1939 was surrounded by evergreens and from the porches we could hear the nearby brook. The villa was on top of a hill, a picturesque site reminiscent of

Switzerland, yet isolated from the hubbub of the village where most families with young children lived. My sister and my little brother were my only companions. I missed being with young people my age. The four students living in our villa had fun with my mother, whose wisdom and humor kept them in stitches, while I felt bored and lonely. This was our first time at this particular resort and I felt angry that my parents had chosen that place without considering the social situation for my sister and myself.

True, the scenery was magnificent! And the air so fresh!

But, while we were saying our good-byes, that pure fresh air was permeated with terrible rumors of unrest in neighboring Czechoslovakia. On the radio we heard talk of the plans of the German dictator, Hitler, to annex Czechoslovakia. The atmosphere was further filled with the screaming, agitating voice of this madman promising the German people that he would conquer all of Europe, starting with his and our neighbor, Sudetenland.

Our family and summer neighbors kissed and hugged and said, "See you next year."

But somehow, because of the rumors of war, we felt we might never see each other again. With our belongings packed we were driven to the train station in a carriage and headed home. Three and a half hours later we arrived at the Bendzin train station where our father was waiting for us.

My father was very happy to see us looking so well upon our return from the summer in the mountains. However, despite his joy at having us home, he seemed very tense and troubled. My father was always a serious man but now he seemed anxious. He shared the news of the possibilities of a war with my mother. Of course we couldn't help overhearing, "A war is a terrible thing. Food is sometimes impossible to obtain. I worry," he said, "about food for the children."

How naïve he was to think that food would be his biggest problem. This was to be a war beyond his or anyone else's imagination.

In late August of 1939, because it was almost time to start the new school year, my mother proceeded to get us ready. She bought us new clothes and notebooks. But there was more and more unrest and uncertainty in town. The prospects of school reopening and normal life resuming were unlikely. Everyone was glued to the radio when the most dreadful news was announced:

"Hitler has annexed Sudetenland-Czechoslovakia and is on his way to Poland!"

Paradise lost!

Chapter 2

FATEFUL DECISION

Because of the announcement of the German invasion plans, after our return from the mountains in late August, my parents tried to decide what to do. Should we stay and face the enemy? Or should we run away to a distant area in the hope that the Polish army would fight back and succeed in defeating Hitler's army? The decision was to run.

So we left our home with a few belongings, such as clothing, bedding, and the food we had in the apartment. My parents told us to wait while they tried to secure a driver with a horse and buggy to take us farther north. They found one, who was willing to do this, I am sure for a large sum of money because the demand was great. Many people needed transportation in order to escape. We climbed into the wagon and rode about fifty kilometers to Olkusz, where the Polish driver left us near a large pile of hay. This was to be our resting-place for the night, and in the morning we would decide what to do next.

We tried to rest through the night, occasionally dozing off. The sky was lit up with artillery, apparently from the battle between the Poles and Germans. Any second, we thought, the bullets would reach us, but by some miracle they did not. However, to our dismay, within a few hours, with daylight, we saw a motorcade of German tanks. The Polish army, ill-equipped, had given up. The enemy had caught up with us and our escape seemed futile at this point.

Why then remain in a strange town surrounded by Germans, when we could be in the same situation but at least in our own home. And so again, my father secured a farmer with a horse and buggy and back we went.

The fifty kilometers back to Bendzin seemed like an eternity. The town seemed very quiet; very few people were in the streets. The farmer left us in front of our apartment house at Pilsudska 13 (unlucky 13) and we were happy to finally reach our apartment where we could rest and sleep.

We climbed to the third floor, unlocked the door, and found everything intact. We couldn't wait to get into our beds for everyone was exhausted. No sooner had we rested our heads than we heard shots burst through our windows. My father ordered us to lie flat on the floor to avoid being hit. Fortunately, no one was physically hurt. But we were terrified.

Voices from outside, carried through a megaphone, announced:

"Alle Juden raus." "All Jews out."

"My God, what bad luck," I thought. If only we had arrived an hour later we could have avoided this roundup. But here we were. We were ordered to march down the street and face the enemy. They commanded the men to separate from the women and children. Without explanation they loaded the men into a big truck, twenty-nine of them, and ordered the rest of us to go back home. I could read the relief on my father's face when he saw his family free to go.

I wonder what was on his mind. Did he anticipate his own fate?

The first crushing blow. Women and children screaming, crying hysterically ...

Will we ever see our father again? What is going to happen to him? The residents of Pilsudska 13 and some from the adjacent buildings went back inside feeling desperate and helpless.

My handsome, intelligent father! He took care of everything. I loved him so much, and even though he was not outwardly affectionate, I knew that he loved my siblings and me and was ready to give his life for us. Who will protect us now?

Chapter 3

MY IMMEDIATE FAMILY

My father Abel Ickowicz, 36 years old in 1939, was a stern man, an intellectual, and a loner. His family was his entire universe. He was an only child; his mother had died in childbirth leaving him alone with his father and a nanny, Leosia, who cared for him like a son. My grandfather eventually remarried a widow with two children and the stories in the family circulated that she treated my father poorly. She was a stereotypical stepmother.

My father was not a religious man, per se, but a very staunch Zionist and a proud Jew. His dream was to eventually go to Palestine with his family. It is this spirit that he instilled in his children. We were proud of our heritage and in case we forgot about it for even a moment, there were plenty of Polish anti-Semites to remind us of it quite often. Name calling, stone throwing, burning fur coats Jewish women were wearing (with cigarettes "accidentally"/on purpose) were common occurrences. No, we never felt truly at home in Poland. We were in the Diaspora, living outside of our homeland.

My beloved parents Andzia (Chana-Gitl), nee Safirsztajn, and Abel Ickowicz shortly after their marriage, circa 1921.

My mother's maiden name was Andzia Safirsztajn. Her Jewish name was Chana Gitla. She was one of eight children born to Joseph and Royzia Gold Safirsztajn. Her mother died shortly before I was born, so I never had a grandmother. I always missed having one and envied my friends, who were lucky enough to have theirs. Quite the opposite of my father, my mother was gregarious and always laughed and joked. People loved being in her presence. I often wondered how these two opposites got together and fell in love. But they had both lived in apartments around the same courtyard and their families knew each other. So fall in love they did, got married and actually complemented each other very well.

My sister, Bronia, the first-born of my parents' three children had an impaired eye muscle and wore glasses. Other kids teased her, because of it. My parents did everything they could possibly do for her. Bronia and I sometimes quarreled, mostly because we invaded each other's wardrobes. We never, however, were cruel to one another or used foul language. That would not have sat well with our parents who were very strict about our manners and about the language we used. Bronia just wanted respect from her little sister, who was not so little and had a mind of her own. She had her friends, and I had mine. How much she cared about me I found out shortly after the outbreak of war.

Curfew was immediately enforced when the German's entered Bendzin and no one was allowed outside after dark. I had gotten together with several of my friends three streets away from Pilsudska, where we still lived. It was so great to forget the war and have a little fun. We lost track of time and did not pay attention to the sunset. Suddenly my sister appeared at my friend's apartment, breathless from running, and ordered me home. I was scared and sorry for putting her in that position. It was dangerous to be in the streets after curfew. As we reached the vestibule and were about to leave the building, she smacked me saying,

"How could you worry us like this. Mommy is so upset."

She was right! We quickly ran home without any incident. As we reached our building, she stopped me for a moment and said,

"I'm glad you're OK. I am sorry I smacked you."

She gave me a hug and whispered, "You know I love you."

"Me too," I whimpered through my tears.

My other sibling, Marek, my eight-year-old brother was the apple of everyone's eye. He was adorable, with a round, sweet face surrounded by dark hair. When he was born, a boy after two daughters, it was as if Messiah had arrived. How happy everyone was with our little Mareczek. It was always I whom Mommy appointed to take my little brother along even though he was in my way when I was with my friends. I was closer in age to him than my sister, therefore, deemed the more appropriate one to hang out with. He was so sweet and so grateful to be tagging along with me. I loved him so much.

I was in the middle, neither here nor there, somewhat hungry for attention, which I mostly got from my aunts and uncles who showered me with affection and attention. I was named after their mother, my grandmother Royza, who died while my mother was pregnant with me.

My dear little brother Marek (Mareczek) at the age of three, during one of our summer vacations in the Beskid Mountains, circa 1935.

Our family was very close and loving and functioned well as a unit. My mother was a gourmet cook who prepared scrumptious meals often consisting of six courses. Throughout the years we always had a live-in Polish country girl who helped with the household chores. Each of these maids would stay for several years until she found a husband. We children were always sorry to see them go for we became attached to them.

Everyday the table was set beautifully with dazzling white linens and fine china as we sat down for our main meal of the day, with our father at the head of the table. This daily ritual of our midday meal was an integral part of our family life.

My father supervised his children's education, exposing us to books and music. We even took private English lessons. My mother loved to hear us recite and converse in English, even though she did not understand what we were saying. She loved the sounds and regarded our recitations and conversations as performances and the fruit of her and my father's efforts to educate us. Together they created a wonderful atmosphere in which to grow up.

We were a middle class family, far from being rich, but lacking nothing. My father earned a respectable living and provided well for his family. My parents sacrificed other things in order to provide the best possible education for us. They considered education their most important responsibility. I was the best student in my class and always had all A's on my report card. Nothing less was expected of me and I loved learning.

> *One day I got an A- on one of my tests and when I arrived home, where the table was already set for dinner, which was eaten at two o'clock in the afternoon, I locked myself in the bathroom and cried. I wanted to evoke sympathy from my father, who came home for the midday meal, so I did not appear at the table. I wanted my parents to summon me from the bathroom and forgive me for the A-. When they saw how upset I was, they did forgive me and assured me that it didn't matter and they loved me anyway.*

These pleasant memories of my youth are precious to me and I am so grateful for having them.

My immediate and extended family in Bendzin, Poland, 1931. The occasion is the marriage celebration (in absentia) of my Uncle Mordecai (Murray) in America. I, at the age of 4, am sitting in front, on my maternal grandfather Joseph's lap. My sister is in the back (under the wall photo of my maternal grandmother, Rojza), held by my maternal grandfather, Shaj. My Aunt Regina Safirsztajn is on the far right. My parents are in the second and third rows center. **I am the sole survivor of my entire family.**

Chapter 4

MY EXTENDED FAMILY

My mother, Andzia, had seven siblings. She was the eldest of the sisters and the first one to marry. The second sister was Tonia, a beauty, who married an unattractive, but very kind man who adored her. The next, Cesia, a sweet, shy and kind soul, had neither the luck nor opportunity to marry, for after my grandfather was widowed, she kept house for him. My youngest aunt, Regina, was a very petite and elegant woman who spent all the money she earned on custom-made shoes and hats. I loved trying on her hats and to this day, I am a "hat person" and am reminded of her whenever I wear one.

My eldest uncle, Mordecai, later known as my Uncle Murray Safirstein (Anglicized version of Safirsztajn), immigrated to the United States with several of his cousins to avoid entering the Polish army. I didn't meet him until I came to America with his sponsorship. My Uncle Ezel, I believe I only knew from pictures. He was gorgeous and wealthy. Before I was born he moved away after an arranged marriage to a girl from Lodz. He and his wife had a son, Jurek. My Uncle Isaac, amusing and intelligent, married a fine woman, a head taller than he, from a neighboring town. They had a beautiful boy, also named Jurek. My youngest uncle, David, the only tall person in my mother's family, was also handsome, and a born comedian. During the war he and his friend were hired to entertain at private parties in the ghetto. They were very funny and brought laughter into people's lives when it was so desperately needed.

My grandfather was the only one in my family with whom we had to speak Yiddish. Although born and raised in Bendzin he never learned the Polish language. He had no need to because he had no contact with non-Jews and his family and friends spoke with him in Yiddish.

We grandchildren, however, spoke Polish with our parents at home. Polish was the official language in school as well as in conversations with friends. I spoke with my grandfather in my limited broken Yiddish, but I knew and understood enough to converse with him.

Later, my Yiddish language skills served me well, enabling me to communicate with my fellow Jewish inmates in Auschwitz. The Jews who were sent to Auschwitz came from many different European countries and spoke the languages of their native countries. In addition, they usually spoke Yiddish, which was really a mixture of many languages. Yiddish was the language of the Jewish people in the Diaspora that made it possible to understand and communicate with each other regardless of one's country of origin. Eventually, I mastered this language very well.

All the holidays were spent in my maternal grandfather's house with the entire family gathered. I vividly remember the Passover Seders so rich with tradition, which started at sundown and ended close to midnight. All the grandchildren routinely fell asleep and were carried home on my father and uncles' shoulders.

The description of my mother's family, the Safirsztajn clan, whom I brought to life on these pages, is my tribute to them. There is not a soul left in this world, except for me, to bear witness to the fact that they and their families actually once lived. But I do think about them, and remember my aunts, uncles, and cousins with love. I am tormented by the unknown, for as far as most of them are concerned, I don't know how or when their lives came to an end. What did they feel and think as they faced death? Were their deaths excruciating? Did they wonder if any of us were still alive? I will never know the answers. But in my memorial prayers I always include them; no one else does. May their souls rest in peace.

Chapter 5

BENDZIN

Bendzin was a town situated on the southwest corner of Poland, bordering Germany on the west and Sudetenland-Czechoslovakia to the south. In 1939 Bendzin had approximately 25,000 Jews in a total population of 40,000. The Jews had lived here for almost 600 years. My own family on my mother's side was able to trace its roots back to the 1600's.

The Nazis annihilated ninety percent of the Jewish population of Bendzin.

Jewish people in Bendzin were mostly merchants, tailors, shoemakers, and peddlers. However, there was also a goodly number of intelligentsia, upper-middle class, a few doctors, and a few wealthy families, who owned factories and manufactured and distributed products all over Europe. One such family was the Gutmans, for whom my father worked as an accountant. Another was Firstenberg; a great philanthropist who built a magnificent school called Gimnazium Firstenberga, which was specifically for Jewish children.

My beloved school Gimnazium Firstenberga in Bendzin. It is still a school to this day, but without a single Jewish child.

It was a private, exclusive school with outstanding professors and faculty and included kindergarten through twelfth grade and graduation called "matura." Children from miles away traveled to attend Gimnazium Firstenburga. It was so prestigious that when one achieved "matura" it was equivalent to completing two years of college education. My siblings and I attended this Gimnazium, and because my father's boss, Mr. Gutman, and Mr. Firstenberg were friends, we received a substantial discount, thus enabling us to have the very best education and learning environment.

I remember when I was seven or eight and had to be in school at nine in the morning, the same time my father had to be in his office. How happy I was to trot on my little feet along side my six-foot-tall Papa, who couldn't help but take large steps. How I cherished those times.

Bendzin was a friendly town. It had its share of poor people who could barely feed and clothe their large families. However, Jewish people took care of their own. A Jewish Kehila—an assembly of elders in the Jewish community—helped the impoverished live a decent life. In most cases, the poor lived in crowded apartments, not in the best areas of Bendzin. Poverty, however, did not necessarily diminish their stature in

The 1938 graduating class of Gimanzium Firstenberga. The faculty is in the top row; most of them were murdered in Lvov. Only a few students survived.

My sister Bronia's class in Gimnazium in 1938. Bronia is in the last row, far right.

My 4th grade class in 1935. I am in the second row, second from the right. I am able to identify all my classmates. Only a handful survived.

the community. If they were good and honest people, they were equally respected. By the same token, there was a division of classes. Money, as everywhere else in the world, afforded one a better life, better housing, better clothing . . . Bendzin was no exception.

In Bendzin there was little contact between the Jews and the Poles. Because we attended a Jewish school, we only had Jewish friends. But, even those who attended public schools socialized primarily with Jewish children. We didn't intermingle. There definitely was a divide between us. Perhaps, because we knew how deeply rooted anti-Semitism was in Poland, we kept to our own and distrusted the Poles—as it turned out, for good reason.

Chapter 6

AFTER THE FIRST STORM

From the time my father and the other men were taken away from us the mood on Pilsudska 13 was one of gloom and desperation. But sometimes there were days when hope and elation prevailed. A fictitious rumor circulated that the men taken out of Pilsudska were seen someplace and were alive and well. We clung to this ray of hope, however unsubstantiated the news was. But, grieving went on and on and never really stopped.

We also learned that while we were fleeing for that short time, during which the Germans entered Bendzin, they had burned the synagogue packed with praying Jews. They caught elder Jews with beards and earlocks and shot them in the streets, leaving the bodies for people to see. Eventually the families claimed the bodies and tried to bury them properly. Yes, this was the way the Germans announced their presence in every town and village they entered.

Immediately, we had to deal with our own survival. There was a food shortage and one of us always had to stand in line for bread or whatever food was offered at a given time. Businesses and properties were seized and Jews were prohibited from attending schools and universities. A curfew was enforced, so we had to be home each evening at dusk. All the Jews were ordered to wear white armbands with a Jewish star on them or a yellow Star of David with Jude written in the middle.

After a few weeks some sense of normalcy returned. We were able to move around more freely and achieved some contact with family and friends. We even met with girlfriends on the main street, Malachowska, which briefly and temporarily gave us a false feeling of freedom.

One day while I was walking with five of my friends, somebody ran over to us and breathlessly said to one of them, "Jadzia, your father has just returned from Kartus-Bereza camp." Jadzia screamed with joy, not believing her ears. Her family owned a bank and under some pretext the Polish government had arrested her father in the beginning of 1939 and sent him to Kartus-Bereza camp, sort of a Devil's Island of Poland, a place from which few ever returned home. They had often done this to prosperous Jews, so Jadzia's disbelief was understandable. But it was true! As the Russians occupied the eastern part of Poland they had freed all the prisoners and Mr. Levinson came home. Beaten, emaciated, but alive! I was so happy for my friend.

Plaque at Bendzin City Hall commemorating the murder of the men from Pilsudska 13. My father was among them. Survivor friends from Bendzin are posing underneath the plaque.

I could not help but think, "Wouldn't it be wonderful if someone would bring us the same good news about my father." After all, we had never seen his body, so we always clung to that little ray of hope that perhaps we would see him again.

Tragically, at the end of 1941, people living in the building adjacent to the City Hall structure, admitted to witnessing the execution of 29 men in the courtyard. We also learned that these 29 men and one woman were buried in a mass grave in the Christian cemetery.

Final crushing news! The Nazis would not even allow us the right to bury our loved ones with their families saying Kaddish, the ritual mourner's prayer.

Often times later, however, we felt it was best that our father did not have to be subjected to further suffering. He was a delicate man and would not have been able to endure it nor survive.

Chapter 7

PILSUDSKA 13
UPROOTED

The house we lived in when the war broke out was on Pilsudska Street. It was built in 1937 and was therefore very modern in structure. It stood on a lovely street. We had moved to 13 Pilsudska Street just two years before from a beautiful apartment at the far end of town. How proud we were of all the new furniture and draperies my parents had bought for that apartment. We had been very happy there, but not long after having moved in, Polish hooligans traveling in a large group threw stones at our windows and shouted, "Parszywe Zydy" ("contaminated Jews"). Those repeated incidents gave my parents reason for insecurity. Most of the Polish people hated the Jews, who despite their 600 year history in Poland never really felt at home. Jews were never even permitted to become citizens of Poland.

Reluctantly, my parents decided to leave our beautiful apartment and move closer to the center of town

Pilsudska 13, the house we lived in. This picture was taken in 1990. The structure is the same, but the façade has changed.

where we would feel less isolated. A new building was going up on Pilsudska Street and my parents secured an apartment there. As soon as it was completed we moved in. We liked the fact that it was closer to school and to my father's work. It was on a beautiful street and was centrally located even though not as spacious as the previous one.

Several of my friends lived nearby and the movie house, Apollo, was just across the street. Oh, how I loved the movies! There were three movie houses in Bendzin. Every Saturday I spent all afternoon in one theatre or another with my friends. I loved musicals and would watch them over and over again. I even dreamed of going to America to be in the movies—every girl's dream. And I had a collection of movie star photos, which my friends and I traded like baseball cards.

It was not surprising that the Germans decided that Pilsudska Street was too good for the Jews. It was the first street to be "cleansed" of Jews to make room for the folksdeutche, Poles of German ancestry, and for German sympathizers.

The general population was also being resettled if they lived in a desirable neighborhood. This was the beginning of the Ghetto. The Germans designated certain areas, certainly not the choice locations, to be occupied by Jews. Fewer and fewer apartments were available and the area was getting more congested. So we left our beloved apartment on Pilsudska Street where we had only lived for two years, happily. My mother tried to hold the family together, but the meager meals that she was able to put together for us were always a sad affair. Daddy's chair stood empty—a constant reminder of our irretrievable loss. With great difficulty we found a small, less desirable apartment a few streets away. Without any male help, we somehow managed to move our belongings, the ones we were able to hold on to, and the furniture that would fit into our new apartment.

It was around this time that my mother's father, who lived with one of my aunts until that aunt married, began to ail. He moved in with us in one of the places we were resettled to in the ghetto. One day he fell to the floor and died. It was my first experience with actually seeing a dead person, and it was a member of my own family. I saw the ritual of his being carried out of the house in shrouds and witnessed this tragic event in my family. But my grandfather was privileged. He died a natural death and had a long funeral procession on the way to his burial in the Jewish cemetery. He was spared the agony of the gas chamber.

In the meantime a Judenrat was formed in town. A Judenrat was a Jewish government within a German government; in other words, a liaison between the Jews and Germans. All the orders from the Germans were presented to the Judenrat, who in turn were responsible for carrying them out. The Germans actually made our Jewish brothers tools in their hands and gave them the task of collecting Jewish gold, silver and other valuables from us, a demand they made frequently. They usually deceived us by saying that the loot was in lieu of sending transports away to concentration camps. We gladly gave them whatever they wanted in order to avoid deportation.

The Judenrat had the dubious honor of satisfying the German demands, for they too were threatened by the Nazis and hoped that perhaps they could save themselves and their families by cooperating. Most of the people who were part of the Judenrat or the Jewish militia found their task painful and unpleasant. They often tried to warn their relatives and friends to go into hiding when an Axtion, an action, was impending. One was fortunate to know people who were privy to information, such as this, that the general population did not have.

While a lot of people were being deported, the people of Bendzin were being pushed into increasingly cramped quarters. To make matters worse, Jews from surrounding small communities were resettled to Bendzin, making housing even harder to secure and food less available. The living area was shrinking and the population was swelling. We were constantly meeting new people whom we didn't know before the war, people from all social and economic circles. We were all Jews, all regarded as Ferfluchte Juden, an inferior race, and we were all condemned to the same fate.

The SS Troops randomly and arbitrarily caught people in the street and sent them away, sometimes never to be heard from again. Despair was felt in every family. Periodically, there were orders to assemble in a large field where selections were taking place and thousands of innocent people were shipped out. With every round up and selection the population thinned out further.

But, such as it was, life did go on. Young people got together and we tried to escape the gloom whenever we could. We sang together, dreamed together, read poetry. We had to do something to escape the morbid reality and uncertain future. There were romantic interludes ... Love was a great outlet for the pain that each one of us endured.

We missed our school and learning. Private tutoring was going on. I taught younger children, passing on the little more knowledge I had, to them. I, in turn, was part of a high school curriculum class conducted by a brilliant student, Arje Hasenberg, who was three

A reunion of school friends in Israel, 1981, Arje Hasenberg, my friend and teacher in the Ghetto, is in the second row, center. He became a prominent lawyer and changed his name to Arje Ben-Tov.

years older than I. That class was clandestine; being discovered could have brought dire consequences, such as arrest, and even worse, deportation or death.

> *Arje Hasenberg survived the war, became a well-known lawyer in Israel and a leader of the survivor community of Zaglembie, the region that Bendzin was a part of.*

And so the days passed, sometimes hopeful but mostly desperate.

My father's Polish nanny, Leosia, who was with him until he was grown, now visited us every day, crying her eyes out for her Abelek, her dear Abel. She was eventually found dead in the courtyard of our new quarters in the ghetto. I am sure she died of a broken heart.

Chapter 8

An Act of Kindness

In the beginning of 1941, I was almost sixteen years old, feeling hopeless, restless, and trapped. I wanted to live life, no matter how brief it was going to be. I wanted to fight back, to rebel, but how. Every time young people were discussing possibilities of doing something courageous our elders reacted fearfully saying that this would provoke the Nazis more and their treatment of us would be even harsher.

One day we learned that a big transport was being brought into Bendzin, to the "boisko," a large field where soccer games took place before the war. Some young people went to the field to see if they could help these poor souls get settled in the new town where they didn't know anybody. I went, too. A very old couple, German Jews, stopped me and begged to take them home with me, as they didn't know anybody. They feared if they remained in the boisko they would be shipped away again, and they were so old and frail. My heart was breaking for them. I knew how small our place was, certainly too small to share with two old strangers. But I was so moved by their plight that I decided to take it upon myself to bring them home. With a pounding heart, I walked these two fragile people to our already crowded apartment to face my mother.

When Mommy saw us she was speechless. She took me aside and demanded an explanation. With tears in my eyes I explained how I felt and why I brought them home. And so, we divided our little kitchen with a curtain. Two beds and a little table were this elderly couple's home. Of course they shared our kitchen stove to cook their meager meals.

They were so grateful to us for taking them in. I felt good about helping them. Unfortunately we lost track of these fine people when we had to move again to even tighter quarters. The couple was either placed somewhere else or was sent to the final place . . . from which no one returned.

Chapter 9

THE GHETTO

In late 1941, when the official ghetto was formed, we had to have some means of employment, which also meant we had to acquire a Kencarte, an affidavit which provided us with food rations and was, in addition, a temporary deterrent to deportation. Bendzin had a well-known uniform shop run by Rosner, a sort of Oscar Schindler, who employed a lot of Jews. Rosner was a man with good motives, who, while wanting to save the Jews, also profited from our labors.

In the ghetto I, too, worked in Rosner's shop, in the Kirschnerei (fur) section. I had no idea how to sew furs, but my co-workers, professional furriers, taught me how to work the machines. I worked six days a week, eight hours a day. I received no salary for my labor. But the Kencarte showed that I was a "useful" person for the German Reich, so I had a temporary exemption from deportation.

And so the Jews did hope. They hoped that the world would learn about Hitler's intentions. The leaders of nations throughout the world should have known of Hitler's "final solution" from his widely published Mein Kampf, a meticulously outlined plan for conquering Europe, achieving "race purity" and exterminating the Jews of the world.

Some people were not content to merely hope, and escaped to Russia. Some survived there, suffering great hardships while others were massacred. News also reached us that most of the faculty from our beloved school met with death in Lvov, near the Russian border, where they apparently fled. Such educated brilliant people. What a senseless, tragic loss!

We never knew what shocking news we would hear when we got up in the morning. Who was snatched out of a particular building to be shipped to a camp? Who was shot in the street at the slightest provocation? We had already started hearing news about Auschwitz, its gas chambers, and ovens.

Where could we go? Was any country willing to accept us? Were any doors open to us?

Every time I drive through the vast empty spaces and countrysides in the United States, I cannot help thinking how happy the Jews would have been to settle in these places and fend for themselves, without being a burden to anyone. We are a very creative, enterprising people, but no one wanted us.

We had no means of defending ourselves, no weapons; we were helpless and scared. Here and there, there was an incident of bravery, but at the cost of someone's life. Worse were the more severe consequences, such as the arrest and deportation of the rest of the family or of neighbors.

And so life dragged on in the ghetto, working in the shops and playing for time and dreaming . . . *the world must know about us, surely they will come to our rescue.*

Another announcement from the Judenrat: The Jews must deliver one hundred pounds of gold or else! Again, we gave, but did not want to part with everything we had, knowing that we would need something for later.

No sooner had they collected the gold, when, only a few days later, they rounded up several hundred people and shipped them to work camps. In most cases there was no further communication between those people and their families, so nobody knew where they were.

As it turned out, the people who were shipped out fared better than those who thought they were lucky by remaining home and not being deported did. Because they were in work camps, not extermination camps, some managed to survive, depending of course on the conditions at the camp, their individual health and, most of all, on luck.

The ghetto walls were constantly moving in closer, making the area tighter and tighter, resulting in people moving to smaller and smaller quarters. Several of my uncles, my mother's siblings, had been caught in the streets, leaving their wives and children without resources. We were resettled to a two-room apartment and rather then sharing it with strangers, all our aunts with their children moved in with us. We were fifteen people living in two rooms.

At this point my mother, famous in our town for her culinary talents, was approached by the Judenrat and asked to cater banquets for them, for when they met with the Germans to negotiate our fate. My mother welcomed that opportunity because she was able to bring some leftovers home to feed our hungry mouths. She worked extremely hard, but she also felt that she had acquired a certain amount of protection for all of us. After all, she was needed.

She also had the recipe for the most delicious cheesecake that she and my aunts baked and sold. Polish farmers, at a very high risk and a very high price, smuggled in the ingredients for the cakes, for some people still had the resources to buy the famous cheesecake. Thus, thanks to my beloved, resourceful mother, fifteen people were fed and lived and hoped for the war to end. Because if the war didn't end, we knew that the Nazis' ultimate goal was the final solution—total annihilation.

Auschwitz and its ovens were a well-known fact to all. Messengers who were part of the underground spread the grim news. And yet, what were we to do? We were like sheep, helpless, following orders. Despite some insignificant resistance, overall submission appeared to be the norm. It is sometimes hard to believe that this was the situation. Later, many people considered us cowards.

However, Hitler's plan was so well thought out, the method so clever, so insidious. He gathered all the Jews, confined them in small areas, took away their relatives, confiscated their homes, stripped them of their possessions, destroyed their health, broke their hearts and their spirits and later . . .

How could these people fight back?

After the war I learned about the many courageous young people who were involved in underground rebellions against the Nazi regime and how many fell victims during their resistance.

Hope diminished with every passing day. Selected apartment buildings were invaded every day, and when we got up in the morning we found our neighbors and friends gone. Who would be next?

In the beginning of 1942, there was unusual news of an offer for a limited number of Jews immigrate to Uruguay in exchange for money. The Underground jumped at this offer. They collected money and chose thirty people in their twenties—the "cream of the crop" of the town's young men and women who were still around—and offered them this life-saving opportunity.

How lucky they were! How happy we were for them! Surely when they reached Uruguay they would do something to save the rest of us.

But, there was no end to the Nazi machinery treachery. After equipping all the young, hopeful people with passports, making it all look very real and legal, we later learned that they shipped the whole group to Auschwitz—straight to the gas chambers.

What devastating news!

> *Later, when we ourselves were in Auschwitz, some of the relatives of these tragically doomed young people recognized the confiscated clothes they were travelling in as further proof of their final destination. Of course, not one of them was ever heard from after the liberation.*

Chapter 10

DEPORTATION

Another winter passed. It was now 1942. Unbelievably we had existed under these conditions for almost three and a half years. Some people fell in love, married, and even produced children. When I saw a pregnant woman, I ached and was angry. How could these people bring more Jewish children into the world for Hitler to murder? At the time, I didn't understand that unintentional pregnancies sometimes happened in marriages. So children were born and brought short-lived joy to their parents.

Even my eighteen-year-old sister was engaged to David, whom she fell in love with when we lived in one of the buildings where we were resettled. My mother made an engagement party with whatever was available. We were so happy for my sister and her fiancé and hoped for a happy future for them. That future, however, was not in their stars.

I was in love with somebody I was working with at the Rosner Shop. How wonderful it felt to experience this feeling of love, despite such clouds of doom hovering over us. Others who didn't have someone envied those of us who did. Our love made each day so much more bearable. We talked and dreamed of the time after the war. We promised that wherever we were we would look and wait for one another.

Spring of 1943 brought more bad news. Bendzin was going to be Judenrein, free of Jews. The sun was shining, the air was fresh, but trouble was imminent. Where would we be sent next, we were wondering. A few days later and order was decreed that we are to resettle to Kamionka, a remote area between Bendzin and Sosnowiec. By now we had very few possessions. We had either left them behind each time we moved, or sold them for food. The housing in Kamionka were little huts, previously occupied by the poorest Poles, but deemed good enough for the dwindling number of remaining Jews.

In the beginning of August 1943, deportation began again. When we got up in the morning we found some of our neighbors and friends gone. The SS took people in the night. But we heard there was some resistance among the population, which delayed the complete liquidation of the ghetto by two weeks.

Who would be next?

On that fateful day of August 23, 1943, we were awakened by knocks on the door, told to dress in our good clothing, take one suitcase each, filled with whatever valuables we still had, and assemble outside, for we were being resettled. Resettled! What a joke! Did they really think we were blind and deaf to the looming reality? I knew where we were going. But I was resigned. I was glad the end was near. I wanted it to come soon because our conditions were unbearable. The end was inevitable. I wanted it to be over.

My aunt dressed my little two-year-old cousin, my namesake Rózia, so beautifully! *Oh, sweet child, you will never know life.* The guard watching her turned his head away when he saw her. Perhaps she reminded him of his own little child and knew where we were all going. He was clearly moved. But orders had to be followed. When they gathered us up, and had inspected all the little shacks that were our homes to make sure no one remained; they told us to walk a mile toward the train station.

Some people who were later found hidden in the bunkers they had built were beaten and forced to join us near the trains. We were standing there for hours. Some people sat on the ground, unable to stand for so long. But amazingly there was no chaos, screaming or crying. Just resignation, or perhaps, in some cases, hope. Hope that we were actually being resettled and would not be gassed.

After hours of being assembled, we were finally told to board the cattle trains with guards pointing and pushing their guns at us, shouting,

"Ferfluchte Juden! Los! Los! Mach schnell!" "Move on! Move on! Make it quick!"

Chapter 11

DESTINATION AUSCHWITZ

The trip lasted several hours. Auschwitz was in close proximity to Bendzin, but, oh, it seemed like an eternity. Each wagon was packed to the brim with people. Mommy, Bronia, Marek, and I were with several aunts and their children. Fortunately, we were all together to share our fate, whatever that might be. There was not enough room for everyone to sit so younger people were standing up. The heat and lack of air were unbearable. The pail standing in the center of the wagon was beginning to fill with urine and feces. The stench was making people nauseous; as a result, they were vomiting. My little brother Marek, frightened, clung to my mother. Mommy had dressed him in knickers and put a cap on his head to make him look older than his age, hoping he would be spared the fate of very young children. We all had double layers of clothing because we could not carry very much with us. This increased our discomfort. It was August and the wagon had no windows, therefore, no air. We were suffocating.

The main gate at Auschwitz: "Arbeit macht frei" ("Work brings freedom"). (U.S. Holocaust Memorial Museum Archives).

Suddenly the train came to a halt! "Austeigen, mach schnell"—get out and make it fast!

Dazed, everyone tried to rise, but many fell back, their legs cramped from sitting so uncomfortably for hours. People tried to help one another; these were our brothers and sisters who had lived together in the same town and who now waited for the unknown. We got out or fell out of the train half dead to face SS men with their dogs and guns pointing at us. Men and women were immediately separated.

Our fates were determined right then and there. With a flick of a finger we were sent either left or right. It soon became apparent which side was bad, as this was where women with very young children and babies were directed, obviously to the gas chamber. My brother went to the side with men whose fate was being determined separately. Some women were ready to leave their small children in order to be allowed to go to work and, hopefully, survive. As young as I was, I could not condone such selfish behavior. How could they abandon their little children? The few who did, eventually lost their minds over this. Most were unable to bear the consequences of one selfish moment when the will to live overpowered their good sense and good character. Many continued to be plagued by this, talking, crying, acting irrationally, and calling out their dead babies and children's names.

A map of concentration camps. Bendzin is to the left of Auschwitz near the borders of Czechoslovakia and Germany (U.S. Holocaust Memorial Museum Archives).

My mommy, sister, two aunts, and I found ourselves on the supposedly good side. One of my aunts who had married my youngest Uncle David, had a one-year-old son who was immediately taken away; she was ordered to go to our side. Another aunt, Regina, who would eventually become a heroine of Auschwitz, joined us. Another aunt, Tonia, went with her two children, Josele, and beautiful little Rózia. Aunt Cesia had finally married before the war and given birth to a boy, another Josele, and lived with her husband's family on the opposite side of town. We never heard from her or her family so we assumed the worst.

The selection was finally over. We were told to march in a certain direction where we saw a big sign over the gate "Arbeit mach frei"—work sets you free. I thought, "Then it is true! We will work and survive and we were a family together, unlike most people who were separated from theirs. How lucky we are. We will help each other survive."

We kept on walking and heard voices and other signs of life. Perhaps the Nazis meant it when they told us we were being resettled. We entered an area with barracks that looked like housing for prisoners. A lot of women with their hair shaved off were sitting in front of one of the barracks singing: "Mama sontanto felice . . ." *I can still remember the tune to this day*. They were singing what I thought was Greek. There was something bizarre about this scene. We found out later we were in the quarantine section of the camp and these women had, indeed, recently arrived from Greece.

We were told to walk quickly to the right for an ent-lausung—disinfection. But before this, the first thing on the agenda was the most dehumanizing experience: we were told to undress and then our hair was completely cut and shaved to the point of baldness, followed by the shaving of our pubic area, with legs spread. All this with Nazi guards standing around, watching, and laughing, while we felt like screaming from humiliation. The Slovak prisoners, who were actually carrying out this task, handed out a few smacks here and there for good measure.

Tattooing our arms followed. My number was 50887 with a triangle underneath indicating Jewish, for a triangle was half of a Jewish star. My triangle looked like a heart and the numbers were unusually large. The whole transport started with 50,000 and ended with 72,000, that is how many women were brought into Auschwitz within a week, not including the ones who went straight to the crematorium. These numbers on our left arms were to be our identity for the next two years and to this day when we meet somebody with a number within this range we know where they came from and when they arrived in the hell called Auschwitz.

When the shaving and tattooing were finished, we were told to march to the sauna for showers. As we walked into this cavernous bath area I was sure that the spigots on the ceiling which supposedly were showers would at any moment release some poisonous substance and kill us. When water actually sprayed down on us a sigh of relief reverberated in the hollow room. It was strangely refreshing after having traveled for hours squeezed into the cattle cars and standing during the selection under the hot sun for so long. The shower was almost humane.

But we were still naked. We could not retrieve our clothes. Surely they will supply us with new clothes. They did. After we dried our bodies with some rags, we were told to stand in line for our attire. From a bin full of dresses, the prisoners in charge provided us with some clothing, randomly selected, regardless of what weight or height we were. A tall girl could get a short dress and a short girl, a long one. After receiving our wardrobe, which in addition to the dress included one pair of panties and wooden shoes, some girls began to trade with others for better fitting clothing. Although I was short, I kept the long dress I had been given and showed some ingenuity, ripping off two ten-inch strips from the bottom. One strip provided me with an improvised bra and with the second strip I created a turban to cover my bare head. My outfit was complete!

But where was my family? Mommy, Bronia, and my aunts? When we finally found each other, we burst out laughing and embraced one another. We were a sight to behold! Tragedy meets comedy!

When we were all finished with our "grooming", we were ordered to follow a Kapo, one of the camp superiors, to a different part of the camp, where we were going to be housed. It turned out to be the last barrack, Block 27. As we approached this barrack, my heart stood still. Beyond the barbed wired wall, which was only about thirty feet from the block stood the crematorium with its tall chimney exuding smoke. Who knew which of my loved ones or my friends' flesh was burning? We were so close that we could feel the stench.

We were quickly distracted by an order to line up in front of Block 27. A German SS woman appeared to supervise and assigned us to different places to work. My mother found favor in the supervisor's eyes, and was chosen to work in the washkiche (laundry), a very "prestigious" job. Mother of course pleaded with the SS woman to include her daughters and sister-in-law in that line of work. She succeeded. We were especially thrilled about being able to stay together. We were still a family, unlike the rest of the people in our barrack. As we later learned, two other mothers from our transport had succeeded in entering the work camp, Mrs. Baum and Mrs. Oksenhendler. My Aunt Regina was assigned to an ammunition factory called Unionwerke. Other women were directed to all kinds of different jobs.

When this process was finished, we were each supplied with a big, red metal bowl that we learned to guard with our lives. These bowls became our most indispensable possession serving both as a utensil out of which we ate our meager food and as a receptacle for our unexpected physical needs.

We then proceeded to walk into the barracks, which contained two-tier bunks attached to one another, stretching all around the room. In the middle of the room, also serving as a divider was an oven-like structure. We all made a run for the bunks, wanting to be near each other. Mommy, Bronia, and I took one of the lower tiers. Thin straw-filled mattresses and flimsy ragged blankets were our only bedding. The weather was still warm; thus cold was not a threat yet. But hunger! Oh, hunger! Hunger was already bothersome to us because we had not had any food the entire day.

Our Block Älteste, block leader, came out of her room, which was at the entrance to the barrack. Her name was Emma, and she shared the room with her mother, Annushneni, a lovely looking woman of about fifty or less. All the Blockelders were Slovakian Jews who were brought to Auschwitz in 1941 and practically built the camp. They went through many terrible ordeals and a majority of them perished. Those who survived, however, became Kapos, block leaders, and were very tough and mean to us newcomers. They expressed their resentment of us who were at home while they were being persecuted, by cursing and even beating us.

We felt very threatened by the Kapos and could not believe that Jewish women could treat their poor Jewish sisters this way. But perhaps this was their way of surviving. Emma, the Blockelder, welcomed us with a few choice words that were more like threats and warnings, to do as she said or else . . . and pointed in the direction of the crematorium. "Now," she said, "you will all assemble for *Zählappell*—roll call—and then you will get your evening rations."

We were starving and so welcomed this announcement gratefully. But little did we know how long Zählappell would last. Standing on the road in front of the barrack we could see that the occupants of the other barracks of the camp were also assembled for Appell. After two hours a buzz of joy was heard; from far off we saw a large kettle being carried by two inmates. Oh, the food is here! Hunger is such a strong sensation. When your stomach is empty you cannot think of anything else.

We lined up for our soup, bread, and coffee. Some pushed and shoved to be near the kettle, only to be smacked by the Blockelder or Schreiberin, (a person who counts and records the numbers of prisoners)—a Polish inmate, named Zosia. The thin soup was ladled into our metal bowls; a small square of clay-like bread was shoved into our hands. What kind of soup was this? What was in it? It tasted horrible but at the same time delicious. Anything was welcome. We bit into the bread and devoured it all. These rations were to last us until tomorrow evening, but I was too hungry to worry about tomorrow, something I would learn to do later. We also later learned that the bottom of the kettle contained thicker soup—which was more filling.

Eventually, people tried to wait at the end of the line to receive the thicker soup. But often by the time they reached the kettle, there was no soup left. You couldn't win.

Now nature called. The latrine was behind our barrack and all of us made a run for it. Some didn't make it in time and wet the only panties they owned. Later that happened to me many, many times. I would try to rinse them out and dry them under the straw mattress, but they never did dry. I either had to go pantiless or wear wet ones, which did not do much good for my bladder. We then all rushed back to the barracks, lights were turned off, and, exhausted, we fell asleep in our new "home."

My mother woke up after awhile. I don't know what time it was, but she was screaming: "Mareczku, Mareczku, Where are you?" She couldn't stop sobbing. Bronia and I tried to quiet her down and assure her, with heavy hearts, that our little brother surely was in the men's camp, alive and well. We huddled together, grateful to have one another. We needed to get some rest, for we would have to get up early for Zählappell and work, whatever that would be.

Chapter 12

AUSCHWITZ
DAILY LIFE

It seemed as if we had just fallen asleep, our bones aching from the hard bunks, when we were jolted awake by the voices of the Schreiberin Zosia. "Wstawadz, aufschtehen, los, los!" Get up, quickly! Zählappell!

We had never undressed that first night, so we did not have to get dressed, but we did have to use the latrines and revive ourselves with water there.

All three of us walked to the latrines, which consisted of long rows of elevated holes that served as receptacles for our human waste. Afterward, we freshened up as best we could with the cold water running from the few existing sinks. We then hurried back for Zählappell. We lined up in long rows. It was dusk and we were chilled, hungry, and tired. We stood again for hours, and eventually, kettles with hot, watery coffee arrived. It was ladled out into the red metal bowls.

How I wished I hadn't eaten the entire bread ration the previous evening. I would never do it again. One had to think about tomorrow. My mother pulled out a sliver of bread she had saved from the night before and handed each of us a piece.

"Oh, Mommy, Mommy, how lucky we are to have you to take care of us." I hugged and kissed her and saw tears in her eyes.

"Sha, Sha, let's not get mushy! We'll go to work and I'll try to get us more food," she said.

The Appell was finally over and Mommy, Bronia, and I were going to the laundry where we would wash linens for the Blockleaders and elders of the camp.

> *At home, we used to take in a laundress for two days every month. The laundress would wash a whole month's laundry by hand, hang it outside, and iron it—there were no washing machines in those days. I hated that time at home but it was a part of running a household.*

Now, my mother was the laundress and happy to do it. She tried to teach us what to do, so we wouldn't lose our good jobs. We weren't good at it. We were two kids who never did these things at home and Mommy tried to cover for us.

At the end of the day, we returned "home" hungry, exhausted, knowing that hours of standing Appell awaited us. But we also looked forward to our evening rations. I thought often, "God, I am so hungry, how will

I endure it? Mommy said she'd try to get us some food somehow. I know she will!"

We continued our day to day life in the same manner, saving one of our rations for the following day. One morning when summoned by the Stubowas—section leaders—to get up, we discovered, to our horror, that the bread was gone. I could hardly sleep, that's how strong my hunger pangs were, but we had learned our lesson about consuming all out food at one time and so we saved it. And now it was gone! I started to cry. I was so angry and devastated. We could have eaten it ourselves, but some dishonest person stole the food that belonged to us.

"No dear," Mommy said trying to pacify me. "The person who did this is not a thief. She must have been terribly hungry! Forgive her." My mother was so wise and kind. During our concentration camp years, we had experienced so many such sad incidents. It was survival and under these circumstances, people were capable of anything. And yet there was a lot of camaraderie among the inmates, especially those that came in the same transport.

Mommy was trying to lift everybody's spirits even as low as hers were. She realized how lost and lonely the young people were without their families. She herself suffered unbearably because of never having heard from or of my brother. As weeks went by, people were able to make some contact with living relatives who were in the male camp. Some men were even coming to our camp and every so often, one would recognize a familiar face and inquire about his or her loved ones.

Mommy dreamed about Mareczek and called out his name every night. Only when I myself became a mother did I fully understand the agony that was my mother's. And yet, she cared for us and supported the other girls . . . how strong she was! And, she kept her promise. She did extra washing and ironing for our block leader Emma and her mother, for which she received extra food, that was a lifesaver. She even brought a sheet for us to sleep on. What luxury! Our underwear was kept clean, and life for us was bearable.

Some people had "posh" jobs in Kommando Canada, which was the best there was. These girls sorted clothing that the arrivals to Auschwitz had been stripped of. Needless to say, their access to these clothes were very advantageous and many of them helped out others with whatever they could. Most of the inmates were helpful to others if they were in such a position.

Some people worked in the shoe Kommando. Many of my friends were among them. There was a Weberei where one worked with leather. There was a nehstube, a sewing shop, where uniforms were fixed. There were Ouserkommandos—work outside the perimeter of the camp—where people walked several miles to reach the site. They were exhausted even before they began to work up to twelve hours a day. These were the worst jobs you could possibly have. Where you were assigned was not your choice; it was your luck and destiny.

Chapter 13

SELECTION

About six weeks after our arrival, we faced our first selection. It was already pretty cool outside, mid-October, when we were told to undress and parade naked in front of Dr. Mengele, the so-called Angel of Death, and other SS men with dogs. Luck was a big factor then. If they did not like your appearance, they pointed their sticks to the left—to death.

Everyone walked erect, smiling, feigning well being, hoping this behavior would convince the SS men. No, they needed to eliminate a certain number of prisoners and it didn't matter to them who the victims were. None of us looked that emaciated yet. That would happen later, with time. Starvation and illness would do its job. But, right now, thirty girls from our block and many, many others from other blocks were selected to go to the gas chambers. The rest of us were allowed to live and continue our miserable existence.

Mommy had a lot of work to do for Emma. And because of the selection, we worked late. When she got Emma's laundry ready, she asked me to please deliver it to her before she went to sleep. "But Mommy, I am so tired and sleepy. I just can't." I will regret those words until the day I die! How could I refuse my poor, hard working mother and let her do the delivery herself. I would never forgive myself for this insensitive action.

Time went on. Bartering took place on Sunday, when we didn't have to go to work. A pajdka—chunk of bread—for a sweater. A piece of sausage for underwear or socks. The wooden shoes left deep wounds on people's feet, causing pain and infection. We were trying to barter for other shoes—too small or too big—it didn't matter. It was a little improvement. In a way, getting a pair of socks or shoes was more important than eating, for they would enable you to walk to work. If we couldn't walk to work, we were useless and ready to be discarded. The socks stuck to the raw flesh and at night were taken off with difficulty, causing the flesh to bleed. If left on, we would never be able to remove them.

A few weeks later, another selection! With new arrivals coming constantly, room had to be made for them. What was easier than again selecting several hundred people and gassing them? And so the Nazis did. And the chimney of the crematorium right over the fence exuded smoke the next day. Who would be next? We felt pretty much protected by our block leader. I think that had we been selected, she would have intervened and picked somebody else in our place. Thank goodness that never occurred and we had no reason to feel guilty for being saved that way.

Most of us started to show the effects of starvation, hard work and lack of sleep and rest. Some already started looking like "Mussellmen"—concentration camp slang for emaciated people. They lost weight, their legs swelled, eyelids and faces puffed up, while the rest of their bodies looked emaciated. Looking like that was a sure ticket to the crematorium, which of course everybody was desperate to avoid. Was this life worth living? Wouldn't death be easier? Later on, I asked myself this question many times. But, for now, the three of us were in pretty good shape thanks to Mommy's extra work and our good jobs.

But our luck, too, ran out. Soon fall passed and winter was at our doorstep. Torturous Appells were more and more difficult. Sometimes we had to support people to prevent them from fainting and falling on the ground. With little clothing, they dragged themselves on the long hike to work. Many times, they were brought back as corpses on a wheelbarrow pushed by their fellow inmates.

Chapter 14

TYPHOID

In January 1944 a typhoid epidemic broke out and more than half of the inmates contracted it. Mommy got sick first and then I became ill. We had very high temperatures and were shivering uncontrollably. Emma, the blockleader, told us to go to the "camp infirmary" called Revier.

> *Some infirmary! There were no medications or treatment for ailments. You just lay there in lice infested bunks, one step away from the gas chamber.*

It was quite a walk from our barrack and freezing outside. I don't know how we managed to get there. When we finally did, there was a long line of sick women waiting to get inside. Apparently, typhoid was rampant in the entire camp.

Mommy and I huddled together begging, "Please, please let us in!" I don't know how long it took for us to get in. It seemed like forever. We were assigned to two bunk beds. I climbed to the top one and Mommy lay down on the bottom one. We covered ourselves with existing blankets and immediately started scratching ourselves. We were bitten alive by bed lice. Mommy was moaning and calling, "Mareczku! Mareczku!"

> *I miss him too, Mommy. I love him so much! Do I still have my baby brother or did he go up in smoke as soon as we arrived six months ago?*

A short time after we settled into out beds full of lice, SS men stormed into the infirmary and ordered everyone to get up. We knew what was coming. A selection! But we were all sick. Why not take the entire Revier and load us on a truck and finish us off once and for all? Nobody budged. The orderlies ran around yelling, "Aufschtehen, los, los."

I decided to stand up and be the first one to go and face the SS man. He wrote my name and number down and pointed me to one side. Is it a good side or bad? I had no way of knowing because I was the first one to approach them. As people kept getting up to face the beast, it was apparent to me that those in bad shape were sent to my side. Mommy, too, was sent where I was. I don't think she knew the seriousness of the situation. All she cared about was that we were together and so did I. At least my sister avoided the selection by remaining on the block. Maybe one of us will be saved.

The "bad" line was getting longer and longer. When the selection was finally over, we expected to leave the infirmary and be loaded into trucks. To our surprise, we were told to go back to our beds.

Had we been dreaming? Was the selection a figment of our imagination? Fever does that to you. A little while later food was distributed to the sick inmates. Most of us were too sick to eat. I remember dreaming about apples. I don't know the reason, but I had this insatiable desire for apples. In my momentary consciousness, I noticed a familiar face lying on the tile stove for the warmth. I called out to her, "Jadzia, is that you?"

She picked up her head and walked over to my bed. "Róziu!" she exclaimed happily.

Jadzia was Jadzia Levinson, whose father returned from the prison Kartuz-Bereza during the war. She told me she had come to camp with her mother, who went with the previous selection. Her younger sister never made it to camp, but she hoped her father was in the men's camp. Too weak to stand, she went back to lie down on the tile stove and went into convulsions. She shook uncontrollably, fell off the stove, and died. What a shocking sight! My dear friend. My poor, dear friend!

Years later, on one of my visits to Israel, I attended a wedding where I saw Mr. Levinson looking well with his new wife at his side. It was painful, I am sure, for him to see me. I reminded him of his daughter Jadzia, but I wasn't going to tell him that I was the last person to see or speak to his daughter. What was the point?

Ironically, because of the war, Mr. Levinson survived and his family perished. I was not going to make him feel any more guilty than I am sure he already did. But Jadzia was lucky in a way. She would not have to be gassed, only cremated. She would not feel a thing. We were the ones that would have to endure the gassing.

Chapter 15

ONE MORE MIRACLE

But when? When were the SS coming to get us? I really couldn't say when they came, whether it was two or three or four days later because I had no conception of time. But, they did storm into the infirmary with their list of victims.

Of course I readied myself to be called first since I was the first whose name was written down. But no, my name was not first to be called. Neither was it the second or the third. Could they be reading the list from the bottom up? What agony! I so wished it to be over. Names, names are called . . . Chana Ickowicz . . . that is Mommy!

"O Mommy, don't leave me! I am coming with you! They will call my name soon!"

Did I say it out loud? Did I think it? Did I wish it or did I hope my name would never be called?

The list is finished. The people are told to walk toward the door and to the truck waiting outside. I hear Mommy's voice crying out to me,

"Róziu, I am going to the gas chamber! **Try to survive and tell the world."**

"I will Mommy. I will try for you, Mareczek, and everyone else ..."

Then they were gone and I was still in bed. How? Why? Who intervened? The orderlies couldn't believe that I was still there. They stared at me with amazement. And, what's more, I was feeling better. My fever broke, but my body was a mess from constantly scratching at the lice. Now that I was conscious, I found the itching unbearable and scratched myself to the point of bleeding. I was given some ointment by the aide, which helped a little. I was beginning to feel hungry—a good sign I was told.

But, I couldn't stop crying. Crying for my mommy, my brother, my father, and yes, for me. What was to become of me? Without Mommy I would not survive. Why didn't I go with her? "However," I thought, "I still have my sister. We'll have each other."

No such luck! While we were at the infirmary, there was a big selection in every block in the camp. My poor sister was taken to the gas chamber then. Now I was really alone. I didn't want to live!

I was ready to be discharged and sent back to Block 27. I was very weak and could barely walk, but slowly and shakily, I made the long distance to the barrack. There I hardly saw any familiar faces. I knew where they had gone. I felt so lonely! It was this overwhelming emotion which completely took hold of me. Even hunger was not the most painful. I lay on the koya-bunk—in a fetal position and cried. I felt abandoned and hopeless. I wished I were dead! What was the point of living?

I never could get over the miracle of my name being erased from the list while I was in the infirmary. Years later, someone I ran into from my barrack in Auschwitz thought that she had the answer. This is what she told me:

When Emma, the Blockelder, learned that my sister Bronia and my mother were definitely to be killed, she somehow learned about me and was instrumental in having my name removed from the infirmary list. She wanted to save at least one of us. I find it hard to believe. Yes, Emma and her mother did favor us, but how could she have known about me?

I believe a higher power is responsible for my fate, as well as everyone else's. Yes, sometimes being enterprising helped. But what counted most was luck. I was meant to live and the only extraordinary thing I did took place later when I escaped from Auschwitz, a story that I write about in a later chapter of this book.

Chapter 16

TO SURVIVE

Emma allowed me to regain my strength and did not assign me to work, but I had to attend Appell. It was so much harder than before when I had my mother and sister and was pretty strong. Now, my physical and emotional state made the Appell almost unbearable. In addition, I, like everyone else that survived typhoid, was plagued with dysentery, the most unpleasant and difficult condition to manage. You could not control your bowels, which had terrible consequences. Also, the scabs all over my body from scratching, called cretze became infected and filled with puss. I lost a lot of weight and was a real Mussellman.

I was lucky to be assigned to the Nehstube, where German uniforms were repaired, but I sat like a zombie with a far away look on my face.

I was later told by the people working there that they thought typhoid had damaged my brain because I looked as if I wasn't "all there." Perhaps it was true at

the time, but judging from my perfect rec-
ollections and what I later accomplished
in my life, I know I did not suffer any
permanent brain damage.

I would say that I was suffering from enormous depression and sense of abandonment. Finding myself all alone, without my mother and sister, was a great shock to my whole being.

The forelady of the shop was very nice to me and overlooked the fact that I did not produce any work. There were no Germans around and the atmosphere was pretty relaxed. At the end of the workday we assembled for Appell, which was very exhausting and there we received our rations. Fortunately, our barrack was just across the road and I had to drag myself there. As soon as I lay down on the koya, I started crying. I wasn't even hungry, but my sleeping partners kept encouraging me to eat in order to get stronger.

Suddenly, I heard a familiar voice calling my name. I guess she was pointed in the direction of my bunk and there she stood before me, my Aunt Regina, with a pint of milk in her hand.

Where did she come from? Was I dreaming? Regina, who was working in the Unionwerke, ammunition factory, did not contract typhoid. She knew about the big selection and somehow heard that Mommy and Bronia perished but I did not. Her factory was far from the camp and their Kommando usually got back after dark. But here she was, exhausted from work, and walking the entire length of the camp to find me, give me the milk, and lift my spirits.

My dear, dear Aunt, how good you make me feel. How grateful I am for having at least you!

Her appearance every other night with either bread or milk helped me physically and mentally. I managed to work and produce at the Nehstube and snapped out of my depression a bit. I looked forward to my Aunt's visits several times a week. I did not know anything about her clandestine activities. Not until after the liberation did I learn about her heroism.

And there was dear Mrs. Oksenhendler who was one of the few mothers who entered the work camp of Auschwitz. She showed me enormous compassion by asking me and some other girls to join her and her two daughters, Regina, and Jadzia, on most Sundays when we didn't work. She worked in the sauna where she was able to cook some soup, which she offered to share with us, a very generous act on her part. She also gave me clean panties to replace the ones I wore out by constantly trying to keep them clean, due to the accidents I had because of my durchfall—dysentery. She also realized how lost and lonely I was since I had lost my mother and sister. She knew us well at home, for my mother bought kosher chickens from her. It was their family business.

This lovely lady lived to a ripe, old age with her husband, who also survived.

They were a unique exception in the Holocaust experience. Many years later, I had the privilege and opportunity to honor Mrs. Oksenhendler for the good deeds and charity she performed under the most inhumane circumstances. May she rest in peace. I'm sure she is in heaven.

Mrs. Oksenhendler's two daughters, Regina and Jenny, formerly Jadzia, have become my lifelong friends. They both live in Canada, have families, and have made successes of their lives. Jenny is a well-known singer and interpreter of Jewish and Hebrew songs. Regina is a very active member of the survivor community.

Left to right: Mr. Oksenhendler, Rose, Ben and Jack Eisenstein on the occasion of honoring Mrs. Oksenhendler (seated) in Miami Beach, 1982.

Chapter 17

WORK IN AUSCHWITZ

One day, while we were working in the Nehstube, Susie, a gorgeous Slovak Jewish inmate, who was in charge of Ouserkommando, stormed in and demanded twenty girls to follow her. I was one of the unlucky ones. The Ouserkommando work was the most difficult and treacherous of all the jobs and many people were brought back into camp as corpses. There were different kinds of jobs within the Ouserkommando. But to begin with, we had to walk several kilometers outside the camp perimeter and our feet were sore and swollen.

One of the jobs I was assigned to was to move railroad tracks from one area to another, a Herculean job even for the strong and healthy. I had just recovered from typhoid and was still weak and plagued by dysentery. We had to line up a foot apart on each side of the tracks, about forty of us, and told to pick them up at the count of three. I don't even know if those tracks were ever to be used, but I know we were there to be tortured.

When we returned "home" the electric wires looked very tempting. Oh, if I only had the courage to go near them, touch them, and end it all once and for all. I felt so weak and cowardly. I did not have the courage that some did. On the other hand, didn't my mother tell me?

"Try to survive and tell the world."

Another Ouserkommando I remember was moving large rocks from place to place. Why? What for? There was no sense to it. It was cold outside and I was falling asleep standing up. I hid behind a large rock, out of the sight of the German guard, hoping to get some rest. I don't know how long I succeeded in doing so when I was startled awake by a whip over my face. I quickly got to my feet in order to avoid further beating and proceeded with the rock moving.

By far, the worst Kommando I was ever assigned to was a slimy, muddy place, where our job was to fill wheelbarrows with mud and take them from place to place. While doing this, we were sliding and falling in the muck, getting covered with it from head to toe. That was the worst experience and I promised myself that if I were ever to be picked again to this Kommando I would not go, no matter what the consequences. But first I thought,

"Let this day be over so I can get cleaned up, have some food, and get to sleep. Maybe my Aunt will come tonight. If she brings me milk, I can barter it for bread. I need solid food. Food. Always on my mind."

After that Kommando, many others and I were assigned to the Weberei. We were braiding narrow pieces of leather that looked like they were going to serve as whips. It was easy work indoors and we were able to talk to one another, recite poems, and dream of freedom and food.

One day on the way to work, we were passing a men's camp. From across the wires, somebody whom I knew yelled, asking if Rózia Ickowicz was part of the group. He threw a loaf of bread across the barbed wire wall and asked the women to give it to me. The bread was handed to me, which of course I divided into as many pieces as I could. What a boost to my morale! Somebody thought about me, even in Auschwitz.

That somebody was the person I was in love with during the last months in the ghetto. He was working in the Sonderkommando, a unit that had the worst job of all. They were the ones who had the burden of removing the bodies after they were gassed and then burning them in the crematoria. Often they had to burn their own relatives and friends. They were only allowed to hold that job for seven weeks. After they themselves were gassed, another group took over their task.

He gave the bread to his brother to deliver to me, for he was unable to do it himself. In the next few days I received a letter from my friend in which he declared his love for me. I read the letter over and over again and it gave me strength, courage, and motivation to live. I read it to the girls who knew him and me from

Bendzin and they envied me. I did feel special and so I kept going. I began to think that perhaps I should try in some way to escape. I thought about it seriously. But, even if it were possible, with all the guards with rifles and dogs watching us, I would be caught. Nobody who had tried it got away with it. They always found the escapees, dragged them back to camp, and hanged them in front of the entire camp.

Several men tried to escape unsuccessfully and a gorgeous Belgian girl called Mala did as well. Mala had a boyfriend and together they planned their escape. They were miles away from camp disguised as Germans and they checked into a hotel where they were discovered and dragged back to camp. Mala cut her wrists before the Nazis had a chance to hang her. Good for her! That is courage!

Chapter 18

DESPAIR

In Auschwitz one day dragged into another, but once in awhile, as with the escape of Mala, an unusual story was circulated among the prisoners. One such incident was the miraculous escape of a friend from the crematorium. Her name was Idzia Lasenga, a beautiful, delicate-looking girl, who attended school with me.

Idzia was picked at one of the selections to go as we called it "to the gas." She was loaded onto the truck with the other victims to be taken to the gas chamber. In the corner of the truck was a barrel into which Idzia climbed. When the truck reached its destination and the girls were pushed into the chamber, Idzia remained in the barrel unnoticed. The German driver returned to Oswiencim, the town proper, outside the Auschwitz camp.

Eventually the driver noticed Idzia. Scared to death, she pleaded with him to let her go free, "Please, please, let me go. I am young and want to live. I am now outside the camp. This is my chance to escape."

> *People living in Oswiencim claimed that nobody knew what was going on right next to them. Didn't they see or hear anything or, for that matter, smell anything? Impossible! For example, this driver who worked in Auschwitz knew and must have told others what was going on.*

The German was almost ready to let her go, but he was afraid to make such a risky decision, so he brought Idzia back to camp. She was taken to Block 11, a punishment block, where her fate was to be determined. Dr. Mengele found out about her courage and freed her from that block, enabling her to go on living. This was indeed a rare occurrence and was written about in the Auschwitz chronicles.

> *Years later, on one of my trips to Israel, I visited Idzia and her husband and we spoke about our past, as we usually do when we get together with fellow survivors. At that time she informed me that she was the last person to see my mother and sister in Block 11 before they were shipped to the gas chamber. She remembered that they had asked her if she had run into me. They were worried about me. She didn't think they knew the finality of this Block. This information from Idzia affected me in a terrible way and I burst out crying.*

Chapter 19

ESCAPE FROM AUSCHWITZ

In the meantime, I was getting stronger, but one day I didn't feel well. With all my might I got up and went for Appell and then to work. I barely made it back to camp, lay down on my Koya, and fell asleep instantly. I never made the evening Appell. When the girls came back to the barrack, they told me that Zosia, the Schreibein went crazy because one person was missing. She threatened all the girls with punishment unless they told her who the missing person was. They knew, but did not give me away. They were kept two more hours at Appell, but would not reveal my name. Name? I had no name. I was a number—50887. Was I that important? Did it matter that much to anybody that one miserable Mussellman was missing?

But, the Germans were very meticulous and Zosia felt threatened by not being able to account for one "number." Did anybody really care? Zosia announced that the person that did not show up for Appell, when found, would get twenty-five lashes at the gate, a cruel punishment that usually left the punished in terrible shape. I was grateful to my sister-inmates for not betraying me, but I couldn't fall asleep all the while thinking how to get out of this predicament.

There really was no way out. I will be found out tomorrow and taken to the gate for my severe punishment of twenty-five lashes.

"No!" I decided I would not willingly submit to the punishment. I decided to leave Block 27 and hide in another barrack. It was dusk and quietly I sneaked outside and ran to the next barrack. I stopped and ran to the next and the next . . . where was I running to? There was no escape. The wires were electrified—I could run into them and get it over with. I looked up and was reminded of the Germans with guns hovering over the camp from their lookout towers, for any unusual movement on the ground. I expected to hear the sound of gunfire any second. But there was silence and I kept running. Suddenly, I found myself near the gate connecting the B lager (camp) with C, out of view from the SS watchdogs. A large group of women were assembled there, apparently ready to be transported out of the camp. I didn't know where the train was going, but it didn't matter.

I attached myself to this group as inconspicuously as I could and found that they were already counted and ready to be loaded onto the cattle car train. I followed into one of them and with a sigh of relief lay down in the corner of one of the cattle cars. I was too tired to think and too resigned to worry about where this train was taking us. For now I avoided the 25 lashes and I was very hungry. When some food and water were distributed and the train started moving I was very relieved. Nobody knew what our destination was. We could be going to some other extermination camp for many others existed in other parts of Poland.

The government and people of Poland were very willing participants in the Nazi's war against the Jews. They had no objection to the building of extermination camps on Polish territory. They cooperated fully.

The trip lasted for hours and hours. Nobody owned a watch, but a whole day and night went by before the train finally stopped.

The first thing we noticed was a building with a chimney! Oh no! From the frying pan into the fire! I guessed the chimneys in Auschwitz were on overload and they had to bring us all the way here to murder us. But at least I created some havoc on my block and I wondered if they were still looking for me. I was concerned for the girls on Block 27 and hoped they were spared punishment. This might be the end of the journey. I regretted again not having died with my mother.

"Mommy, I really tried to survive, but I am so tired, hungry, and lonely. Hopefully, the end will come soon."

I didn't grasp it at the time, but, in reality, I had escaped from Auschwitz.

Did I realize this at the time? No. I merely wanted to avoid the twenty-five lashes I was to be punished with. It was not until many years later that the enormity of this step and the difference it probably made in whether I lived or perished occurred to me.

Years later the Steven Spielberg Shoah Foundation interviewed me. While relating this incident I stopped and realized the importance of this turning point in my life. Whatever happened after that,

I had escaped from Auschwitz!

Chapter 20

BERGEN-BELSEN

The place where I wound up was another infamous camp, Bergen-Belsen. The crematorium was inactive, which was good news. There seemed to be a lot of chaos, not like in Auschwitz. There were people everywhere.

Where did these people come from? Perhaps I'll see somebody I know who knows her way around here.

Suddenly, as if my prayers were answered, I noticed a friend, Rachela Zelmanowicz, who was part of the orchestra in Auschwitz, which played while people were marching to work. A frail girl, she played the triangle in this orchestra which was headed by a French prisoner, Fanny Fanelon.

Fanny's orchestra experience, under these bizarre circumstances in Auschwitz, was depicted in the movie "Playing for Time."

After the liberation, Rachela and I laughed about her musical talent and were grateful because the triangle proba-bly saved her life. She later became my cousin through marriage. Rachela sadly passed away several years ago, but lived happily until then with her husband, two children and grandchildren, in Israel. We maintained a closeness through the years.

As soon as Rachela saw me, she handed me a pencil and pad and said, "You will count the people and you will be the Schreiberin." She then led me to some other friends who had been deported from Auschwitz to Bergen-Belsen several weeks before, and had already managed to take charge of one of the barracks. One of those people was Sarah Landsberg. Sarah and her family were deported from their native Germany to my home-town of Bendzin in 1938. At that time I took her into my circle of friends and made her feel a part my group. Now it was her opportunity to do the same for me.

Sarah gave me food, which was scarce; she and others depended on girls who worked in the kitchen to provide them with potatoes or scraps of food they could pilfer. They were willing to share with me. Sarah also asked me to stay in her barrack and assume a Sztubowa job. I was happy to be among caring friends.

Sarah survived the war and lives in Israel with her family.

It was the beginning of January 1945 and life for me was easier than in Auschwitz. Unlike Auschwitz, Bergen-Belsen was not a well-organized concentration camp; there was no real German supervision at the time. It was just "survival of the fittest." We former Auschwitz inmates, who went through typhoid and dysentery, were the stronger ones while deportees from elsewhere were falling like flies from starvation and sickness. Bodies were lying around everywhere and stronger prisoners had to pick them up by the arms and legs and throw them into ditches. Transports were arriving practically every day and the people were wandering around dazed. The new arrivals slept on the floor in the barracks, which were not even equipped with bunks.

I often tried to go to the area where the transports were arriving to see whether anybody I knew was there. One day, I noticed my school friend, Marysia, and her mother in the transport. I called out to her and happily she responded. They were being taken to Entlausung, a disinfection center, as all the newly arrived prisoners were required to do. Marysia had a small bag with valuable jewelry, which she had managed to hide, save, and bring from the previous camp. Knowing that she would have to give up her clothes and her bag, I suggested that she give me the jewelry for safekeeping. She agreed. I waited for her to come out of the Entlausungs Kammer and returned the little bag with jewelry to her.

Marysia and I lost track of each other in Bergen-Belsen but found one another forty-five years later and recaptured our friend-

My friend Marysia and I at the Holocaust Memorial in Miami Beach.

ship. She told me that the jewelry secured a good job for her mother and her in the infirmary, taking care of children. Children? I wasn't even aware that Jewish children were allowed to live in the concentration camps. Eventually, typhoid broke out in the infirmary, all the children became sick, and nearly all of them died. Marysia and her mother also contracted typhoid. Her mother died. Marysia survived.

Chapter 21

LIBERATION

The news from the war front was very encouraging. The Nazis were definitely losing the war. But would anybody survive if it lasted much longer? People were arriving from Auschwitz having walked for six weeks in what is now known as The Death March. Many people collapsed along the way or were shot by the guards when they no longer could walk. Had I not attached myself to the transport that left Auschwitz, I would have been in the same predicament. Now I was strong and recovered from typhoid whereas many people were dying from the rampant disease in Bergen-Belsen. The ditch where the corpses were discarded became a huge pile of bodies, which eventually numbered 25,000.

With every group arriving from Auschwitz I looked for familiar faces and recognized many. But not my aunt. Where was my Aunt Regina? Had anyone seen her? The girls kept looking at one another and shrugged their shoulders. Not everyone kept track of who was where. They had their own problems. She'd show up eventually, I knew, and we'd be reunited.

Somebody called my attention to a distant cousin whom I had never met because she lived in a different town. Her name was Cesia, a little girl, a few years younger than I. She latched onto me, and I, willingly or not, became her caretaker. Then another distant cousin, Sonia, showed up. (I knew her because, even though she lived in a faraway town, Lodz, she used to visit her aunt in Bendzin.) She, too, counted on me. After all, they were my relatives, somewhat removed, but still related. And so, I shared whatever I had with them. But they both contracted typhoid and that became difficult. They would not go to the infirmary and lay on the floor, burning up with fever. I tried to ease their suffering as much as I could, but it took time to recover from typhoid.

> *Sonia and Cesia both survived the war,*
> *I'm happy to say.*

Suddenly, a commotion erupted in the camp. The German guards followed one another and started walking toward the exit of the camp. *What's going on?* Something was happening. The Kapos were joining the guards and leaving too. *Were we also free to leave?* We suspected that the guards and Kapos were leaving because the camp was mined and would explode soon. *What should we do? Should we leave too?* We were free to do so, but to follow our enemy and be part of their entourage was not an option. Besides, my two cousins were still sick and I could not abandon them. Some prisoners left, but I and most of the others stayed and waited. Something was happening. We walked near the exit for a sign.

From far, I saw a tall silhouette in a cape and beret. I thought, "It's my father!" He looked just like him from afar. Or, was it a mirage?

After all, I never really saw my father dead and there were rumors that the men from Pilsudska 13 were led away someplace. *Now he has come to liberate us!* Through a megaphone his voice came, "Prisoners, stay where you are! The British Army is here to free you!" And when he came closer and closer, I realized this was not my father. My imagination did that to me. It turned out to be a forerunner for the British Army, which arrived soon after.

We are free! We are free! What do we do now? It came so suddenly. It was—we found out—April 15, 1945!

Our Liberators, the British Army were shocked with what they found in Bergen-Belsen: the mass grave that exuded stench from the decomposing bodies; the half dead lying around with eyes open, pleading for help. They seemed to know we were liberated, but for so many, help came but too late. There were a handful of German guards left behind in camp. I guess the "big wheels" who left did not bother to look for them and take them along. The British gathered up the Germans, stripped them of their guns, and loaded them into trucks. As they were led away, we started screaming at them, throwing whatever we could find on the ground in their direction. Was this our revenge? Perhaps if we had guns, we would have aimed those at the German. But shoot them? I doubt it. Very few of us were capable of killing another human being. But who knows? I was glad we were not given the opportunity.

The British were very kind to the prisoners. They set up tents with beds and, together with the Red Cross unit, proceeded to pick up the sick lying on the ground, and put them on the field beds they set up. There was food available for everyone, but unfortunately the shrunken and sensitive intestines could not tolerate the rich food, which they so anxiously devoured. The result was devastating and people were dying of dysentery.

The next course of action was to liquidate the concentration camp and transfer us to regular housing. They placed us in a group of buildings in the vicinity. I don't know who the occupants were before, but the Bergen-Belsen Displaced Persons camp was thus created. Some very ill people went to Sweden, which offered to nurse them back to health. What a wonderful gesture on the part of the Swedish nation.

Chapter 22

FREE BUT ALONE

The rest of us roamed freely, looking for relatives, friends, and familiar faces from our hometowns. Signs were posted everywhere. Some people came from other areas that were already liberated in search of relatives. Others left camp to return to their hometowns only to find Polish people living in their homes, giving them a cold welcome and a disappointed reaction to their return alive. Occasionally, surviving relatives found one another, overjoyed, but saddened by the loss of the rest of the family.

I stayed in Bergen-Belsen. As one of few survivors who spoke some English, I was immediately recruited to be an interpreter for the frustrated English who could not communicate with the survivors. As I previously said, my parents had insisted that my sister and I take English as an additional language and often ordered us to "perform" by conversing in English. They loved to listen to us! And now, my meager knowledge of the language made me important enough to receive extra rations and goodies like sardines and chocolate. I was also given a nice room and I took in my two cousins and one girlfriend to share it with me.

In June, another distant cousin, David, appeared in Bergen-Belsen en route in searching for his siblings. He asked me who was alive from my family to which I replied, "You know that my father was killed in Bendzin right at the beginning of the war, my mother and my sister were gassed in Auschwitz, my little brother we never heard from after we arrived in Auschwitz. All my uncles as far as I know are dead. All my aunts, except for my Aunt Regina, are dead as well. I am waiting for Regina here, because if I leave, we may miss each other on the way."

"What?" he asked, "Don't you know what happened to Regina?"

My heart pounding, I answered, "No."

After a short pause he said, "She is dead. She was hanged in Auschwitz on January 5th together with three other girls." I burst out crying not believing what I had heard. My last hope for the only member of my family to be alive was gone! I was truly all alone in the world. I wished I were dead too!

Now, the silence of the girls arriving from Auschwitz when I questioned them about Regina made sense. They did not want to be the bearers of crushing news. I could not blame them.

I hadn't known about my aunt's heroism and clandestine activities in Auschwitz. This is Regina Safirsztajn's story:

Aunt Regina was one of the participants in the Sonderkommando uprising in Auschwitz on October 7. For eight months, she had worked in the Unionwerke Ammunition Factory, where she and the three other women involved had access to explosive powder. Regina, together with Ala Gertner (also from Bendzin), Roza Robota, and Estusia (Ester) Wajcblum, smuggled bits of powder in the seams of their dresses and in specially sewn pockets of their clothing. They passed them on to members of the Sonderkommando whose plan it was to blow up one of the crematoria, which would then lead to an uprising in the camp. It was a very secretive and dangerous operation with the Sonderkommando. The four women agreed to this dangerous mission and suffered the consequences. But, I am sure they had no regrets.

The uprising was not as successful as planned, but they did blow up one crematorium and shoved one *SS* man into the oven. The Nazis then proceeded to investigate the whole matter to find the source of the ammunition powder. They started with beautiful Ala Gertner who, despite being tortured mercilessly refused to give any information about the involvement of others. Nevertheless, the SS eventually implicated Regina and the two other women. The whole Sonderkommando was to be gassed as well.

Monument in Yad Vashem, Israel, of the Martyred Heroines of the Auschwitz uprising. The sculpture is of four women, one of whom is my Aunt Regina.

On January 5, 1945, 13 days before Auschwitz was evacuated because of the approaching Russian army, the entire population of the camp was ordered to stand outside where the gallows were waiting to hang the four women and forced to witness their executions. Aunt Regina, Ala, Roza, and Ester went to the

Picture of four heroines currently displayed in Auschwitz. Regina's picture is inserted in the frame on the right, thanks to the efforts of my cousins.

gallows with their heads held high. They died heroines trying to fight back.

Contrary to the general consensus that the Jews went "like sheep to the slaughter", there was resistance—they did fight back. Also, the Sonderkommandos refused to be gassed and attempted to escape. More than 500 of them were shot before the Nazis had the chance to gas them.

> *I am so proud of you Aunt Regina and will never forget you and neither will the world. There are monuments in Yad*

Vashem, Israel, and Germany and articles in the annals of the history of Auschwitz, which hail these four women and the Sonderkommando of the uprising as heroes.

Chapter 23

NEW-FOUND COUSINS

Because of Regina, years and years later, I experienced something that had a great impact on my life. I met a second cousin Lou Murawiec and his wife Betty, who live in Paris, France. I had never known them or heard of them. Lou's mother, first cousin to my mother and Regina, was caught in the streets of Paris by the Nazis, during their occupation of France, and was shipped to Auschwitz. Luckily she returned home alive to her husband and two children, who went into hiding during the war. She was a traumatized woman because of her incarceration, magnified by witnessing the hanging of her cousin Regina. It was not until much later that she was able to talk about the Holocaust with her husband and two grown children.

Lou and Betty, who are seasoned travelers went to Auschwitz, where they saw framed photos of the heroines of Auschwitz. The only problem was that Regina's frame was just that—a frame without a picture. The painful sight made them undertake the tremendous

From left to right: Leon, Rose, Lou and Betty Murawiec, holding: the letter to the U.S. Holocaust Memorial Museum; an award given posthumously to Regina Safirsztajn and the other three heroines of the Auschwitz uprising; and a prewar picture of my family from which Regina's picture was extracted and placed at the Auschwitz memorial.

task of finding someone who possessed a picture of Regina. They wrote to the U.S. Holocaust Memorial Museum in Washington and requested that they seek out some survivors from Bendzin, who might possibly have Regina's photo.

I did not receive a letter, but a lot of recipients made the connection with me. They had witnessed the hanging on January 5, 1945 in Auschwitz and knew I was her niece. I received several phone calls and was given the letter with the plea, address, and telephone number of

Registry of Jewish Holocaust Survivors

Request for Third Party Contact

As a policy we do not provide visitors with survivors' addresses and telephone numbers. This information remains confidential in order to protect their privacy. However, we will forward this form with your message to the survivor.

Please note: The more detail you provide in your message the more likely the survivor will respond.

Date: December 13, 1994

Name of Survivor you wish to contact: Dear Bedzin Survivor,

Dear Survivor,

The family of Rivka Leah ("Regina") Safirstein, executed at Auschwitz on Jan. 6, 1945 for her heroic act with Rosa Rabota and 2 other women to help blow up a crematorium, is searching for anyone who might help us find a picture of her, or information about her so that her act will not be forgotten. She was the daughter of: Josef and Rosa Gold Safirstein. Her sisters were called: Chana-Gitti and Tonia. Her brothers: Mordechai, Tsirel, Isaac, David, Jehudah and Adek. Grandparents: Meir Berich Safirstein and Bronia Trapper.

Please call collect or write until January 7, 1995 at address in New York. After that, call collect or write in France.

Sincerely, The Murawiec family

Your Name: Lana and Laurent Murawiec ℅ Alexander

Street: 61-5 245 Place

City: Douglaston   State: New York   Zip: 11362

Telephone: (718) 225 6093   France. 7, place des Colonnes
                              95800 Cergy
Phone 33-1- 30 31 29 53

Letter written by cousins to Holocaust Memorial Museum in Washington in search of Regina's picture.

my dear newfound cousins, who so magnanimously undertook the task of finding Regina's picture.

I immediately called New York, where their son Laurent and his wife Lana lived at the time. No words can describe how elated they were to hear the news that their search was over. The dear people had never even met Regina, or me, yet they felt as if they had found the biggest treasure.

How did I happen to have a picture? After all, I was stripped of everything when I arrived in Auschwitz and did not have any photos of anybody in my family. Fortunately, my Uncle Murray (Mordecai), the only member of my family who escaped the Holocaust by coming to America, had family photos he had received from his relatives before the war. He was happy to give them to me.

But that was just the beginning of a three-year process of cutting out the small image of Regina from a group picture and getting it to a stage where it was suitable to fit and fill the blank frame in Auschwitz. My cousins maintained constant contact with the museum there. Finally, a phone call from France, "Mission accomplished!" How happy and grateful we all were.

I have since met and gotten to know my cousins well. They have visited us several times in the states. When I first met them, I felt as if I had known them all my life. I will be grateful to them for what they did for my heroic aunt and their cousin forever!

"I love you very much, dear Lou and Betty"!

Chapter 24

AND NOW . . .

With my hope of finding any members of my family alive shattered, I had to decide what to do with the rest of my life. David, the man who informed me about my Aunt's fate, asked me to come with him to Schwandorf, a city in Germany in the American zone, where a transit building for survivors was set up by American personnel with the help of survivors. The German mayor of the town was also very cooperative under the circumstances and provided survivors with beds, mattresses, and anything they needed.

I decided that, since I had no place to go and nothing to do, I would go with David. We traveled by train for many hours and arrived in Schwandorf. The place was buzzing with survivors coming, going, searching, and some staying. Signs were posted on walls with their names and the names of those they hoped to find alive. In a way, I felt like I was part of a community, a community of people who, like me, suffered enormously, lost everyone and everything, and didn't know

in which direction their lives would go. I was amazed
to learn how many different camps people came from.
We had no idea that there were so many.

I was given a nice room by myself and tried to help
around the kitchen. I had no reason in the world to
return to Bendzin and so I stayed. It was June already, I
was eighteen and a half and reasonably healthy, but
terribly lonely.

> *I have been plagued with the feeling of*
> *loneliness all my life. In spite of my zest*
> *for life, good sense of humor, and ability*
> *to laugh, all traits I inherited from my*
> *mother, deep down I became and*
> *remained a depressed person. At times,*
> *later in life, I availed myself of psychi-*
> *atric help. Who could help me? I know*
> *all the reasons for my loneliness and*
> *depression and no psychiatrist in the*
> *world can cure my ills or tell me that my*
> *past was not the reason for it.*

One day, a man from Bendzin named Lajbek Rechnic
stopped in Schwandorf. He was a well-known violin
virtuoso, and I had met him once during the war when
he came to buy cheesecake from my mother. He was
married to a beautiful girl and they, unfortunately, had
a child during the war. He knew that they had perished together in Auschwitz, but was hoping that perhaps his siblings were alive. He had a married sister
with a child and a brother, a doctor, who escaped to

Lajbek Rechnic, as a 16-year-old Violin Virtuoso, 1930.

Russia. His brother did survive in Siberia and later, looking like a skeleton, was reunited with Lajbek. His beautiful sister Helen, an accomplished pianist, perished with her boy. Lajbek and I somehow connected and embraced. I hardly knew him, but he was a familiar face who knew my parents. I guess I was looking for love and, at the same time, a father figure.

Lajbek was twelve years older than I, and very good looking, although he barely had any hair at the time. He was just recovering from typhoid, which caused hair loss, but in time his hair grew back. Lajbek came from a very good family and my parents would have approved of him. But, what if his wife turned up alive or maybe his child was saved somehow? It was only a few months after the liberation and people were turning up unexpectedly alive here and there. A very remote possibility and, yet, a thought that was disturbing. I wished them to be alive. I wished everybody to be alive, but what position would that put me in?

We continued to see each other and after six weeks decided to get married. Mr. Jacubowicz, who was in charge of the little survivor community, organized everything necessary for the wedding with the cooperation of the German mayor who, at this point, was eager to do anything for the Jewish people who remained.

> *During one of my visits to the Holocaust Resource Center at Stockton College, a young man walked in and was introduced to me. This student's last name was Jacoby. Instantly, I connected Jacoby with Jacobovicz and asked him whether his grandfather's first name was Zelig. He said. "Yes!" Excitedly, I showed him the page where I wrote about our wedding in Schwandorf which his grandfather, Zelig Jacubowicz, who became Jacoby, arranged. This meeting had a big impact on me, and I hope, on his grandson.*

It was a huge affair. Everybody was invited to this first wedding of two survivors after the liberation.

Guests included government dignitaries and CIA personnel who were the only people with cameras. They promised to send us wedding photos, but sadly, we never received any.

There was music and dancing and joy expressed by survivors who came from surrounding areas to celebrate and bring little gifts for the bride and groom. Throughout my life, I have met people who were at my wedding. They remembered me but I, of course, did not know the five hundred strangers who were there.

Was it possible for Lajbek and me to know happiness after all we had gone through? Would I be able to have children? It was rumored that the Nazis had put something in our food to damage our reproductive systems. Now that I'd survived, I wanted all the things that human beings are entitled to.

I would go on living, but as it turned out, would never overcome my past, could never stop talking about it with my fellow survivors. We never would get over a trauma such as ours. I never stopped feeling lonely. "Abandoned" first by my father, then my mother, sister, brother, and finally by my aunt. I never stopped feeling guilty for having survived when they did not! But now I had a husband to share my life with, one who could understand me because he had been there. Oh, had he ever!

Chapter 25

LAJBEK'S STORY

Lajbek Rechnic, the man I married, was born and raised in the same town as I, Bendzin. His father decided that one of his sons, the elder, Beno, was to become a doctor and his young one, Lajbek, a violinist.

For a Jewish boy to get into medical school in Poland was impossible. So Beno was sent to Italy, where he entered Padua University.

Lajbek Rechnic, at the age of 22, 1936.

Lajbek traveled every day after school to the music conservatory in Katowice, a half-hour train ride from Bendzin. He really showed great promise and at the age of sixteen was performing concerts. His father made him practice several hours a day and his son obeyed. He studied for

My father-in-law, Markus Rechnic, circa 1900.

My mother-in-law, Elka Rechnic (nee Zelmanowitz), circa 1900.

Lajbek's sister Helen with her husband, son and their dog. Bendzin, 1935. Helen's husband survived the war.

My husband's beautiful first wife, Rózia Borenstein Rechnic. She is wearing an armband with the Star of David on it, the required identification for Jews.

years, but also earned money by playing in a private club for the dining and dancing pleasure of the patrons.

When the ghetto in Bendzin was liquidated Lajbek's wife, child, parents, sister and her family were assembled with everyone else to be "resettled," Lajbek was sent to Zwangs Arbeitslager Annenberg, a work camp, and spent time in the Valdenburg, Buchenwald and Gross-Rosen concentration camps. He was a rather delicate man who never did any physical work. It was unlikely he could endure the hardships that prisoners were subjected to. But luckily, he had a gift that the Nazis found attractive.

As soon as he informed them that he was a Geiger, a violinist, he was given a violin and was on call whenever the Germans had a party, orgy, or wanted to be entertained. Most of the time, it was late at night so he was exempt from going to a regular Kommando. Moreover, he got extra food rations, from which his buddies also benefited.

Once, at the end of 1944, a friend asked him to try and get a letter to somebody on the outside. Lajbek had more contact than the average inmate and succeeded in giving the letter to a Pole who was going to mail it to the right party. Unfortunately, the man was caught with the letter and when questioned about who gave it to him he said, "the Geiger". Well, the Geiger was easy to find and so, within a few days they came, arrested Lajbek, and told the other prisoners that he was "going to Moses," which meant he was going to be executed. They put him into a prison outside of the camp where he awaited his execution.

The war was going badly for Germany and the Russians were approaching. Within a short time, in January, hours before Lajbek was to be executed, they released the prisoners and made them follow the inmates from other camps on the infamous Death March. A miracle!

But, the weeks of marching took a toll on everyone including Lajbek. He could not walk anymore. But, his

Leon and I shortly after our wedding on August 5, 1945.

wonderful friends dragged him and forced him to go on when he begged to be shot. During the Death March he and others were brought to another camp where he met a Polish prisoner whom he knew when he played in the orchestra while he was in the Polish army. Lajbek shared his predicament with the Pole, hoping to get some help. This Pole took him to the morgue where he removed a tag from a dead person and replaced it with Lajbek's tag. Lajbek was not tattooed, but wore a metal tag around his neck for identification. This declared him officially dead. The Germans would not be looking for him any longer to hang him as planned.

The American liberators found Lajbek sick with typhoid on the brink of death. He slowly recovered and when he ran into me in Schwandorf, he was not yet a picture of health, to say the least. But I remembered him when was very handsome and played the violin.

How romantic he was. He composed a love song for me and presented it to me as my wedding gift. He didn't have much else but that meant more to me than anything. We were both penniless and stripped of all worldly possessions. All we had was each other and hope for a new start.

Lajbek wrote the notes and the beautiful words and put them in an album with a note that said, "This is the first of many love songs that I shall write for you! Your loving husband."

Chapter 26

BAYREUTH

Schwandorf was just a transient place. Therefore, Lajbek and I were looking for someplace in Germany where a lot of survivors had settled. Bayreuth, we heard, was just such a town. We packed our few belongings that we had already acquired and traveled by train to Bayreuth. The train was for human beings and we were free! A fact still so hard to accept.

We arrived in Bayreuth and were directed to a street and house that the survivors occupied. They welcomed us warmly and secured a large room for us in the adjacent building. In the next week we became friendly with many of our fellow survivors, none of whom we had known before. We became each other's brothers and sisters—the ones most of us had lost.

We saw some operas in the beautiful Bayreuth Opera House, which was an exhilarating and new experience for most of us. But none of us wanted to remain in Germany. It was just a matter of time as to when we would leave, and where we would go—

Left to right: Lajbek's brother-in-law Paul Borenstein (Rózia Borenstein's brother), Rose and Lajbek in Bayreuth, 1945.

Palestine? The United States? Whatever country would have us.

People were still searching for surviving relatives and wandering from town to town. One day Lajbek's first wife's brother appeared at our door. A young, handsome man, Paul, was the sole survivor of his family. He had heard that Rózia Rechnic was alive, and he followed her tracks. You see, coincidentally, Lajbek's first wife's name was Rózia, like mine. Paul came to Bayreuth hoping to find his sister. Instead, he found me. My heart ached for him. Although only a year younger than I, he appeared childish, lost, and vulnerable. I never knew him before, but I felt his loss profoundly, so my husband and I welcomed him to join the two of us, and we became his "parents."

I grew to love Paul, like my brother, and I hope he feels the same way. He is a sweetheart! When we left for America we promised to send for him, a promise that we fulfilled a few years later. In 1948, we already had two little girls and lived in Queens in a small two-bedroom apartment. When Paul arrived in 1949 we were happy to receive him with open arms.

His bed was a cot in the children's room. He slept through their crying at night, diapered them, played with them, and loved them. And they loved him back; he was their Uncle Paul.

Then along came Dottie Camhi, a lovely American young woman, who rescued Paul from sharing a room with his two little nieces. They soon married, and we were the proud "parents" who gave him away. Dottie and Paul have three children of their own, and they are my children's cousins.

> *When people ask my children how they are related, they try to answer in a brief way, but it is too complicated. All that matters is that we are part of each other's lives forever!*

Chapter 27

IMMIGRATION
TO THE UNITED STATES

Everybody was trying to connect with any living relatives they had anywhere in the world. My husband had some cousins in what was then Palestine, who went there as pioneers before the war. We both loved the Jewish homeland and grew up with love for Zion. Also, Lajbek thought that, as a musician, he had a better chance of furthering his career in a small, growing country.

But I yearned to meet the only living relative that I had, my Uncle Mordecai (Murray), and he was in America. My flesh and blood, my only connection to my mother and her family. I was also hoping that my uncle would welcome the only survivor of his entire family with open arms. In my letter to him, I assured him that we would not be a burden to him in any way. We were young and willing to work for a living in that golden land that gives everybody a chance. To our

"Coming to America". On our way to America in September 1946. On the far left is Lajbek's brother, Dr. Beno Rechnic. Lajbek is next to him. Rose is in the center holding a bouquet of flowers.

great joy we received papers to go to the United States.

On September 16, 1946, we boarded an American military ship, *Marine Marlene* in Bremen-Haven, the second ship to bring Holocaust survivors to the United States.

It was a long treacherous trip. Men were separated from women. We were constantly throwing up. My being four and a half months pregnant didn't help the situation. Finally, after a two-week journey, we arrived in New York Harbor. We gathered our belongings, dressing in our best clothes, so that we would look respectable. As we walked off the ship, the Statue of Liberty stood tall before us! Goldene Medina, the land of plenty, where the streets were supposedly paved with gold. I could hardly contain my excitement.

Will my uncle be waiting for us? How will I know him? Excited, we walked down the ramp and there was my uncle! He looked just like my Uncle Isaak and I could have picked him out anywhere. I started crying uncontrollably and ran into his embrace. I felt a deep love for him and was hoping he felt the same about me. I think he did, but his wife Aunt Sally, beautiful and elegant, had her own large, extended family with whom she was very close, so it was difficult for her to include us. It wasn't my uncle's intention to ignore us, but he wasn't wealthy and his wife's needs were huge. He did buy me a maternity wardrobe in Lane Bryant's and then gave me a job as a finisher in his fur store where he paid me $35 a week, a big help.

Meanwhile, my husband was looking for a suitable apartment on the Lower East Side, the only place where the HIAS organization was remodeling uninhabited apartments for the newly arrived refugees. He found one on the last street, right next to the East River.

Our own apartment! Never mind that the toilet was in the hall and shared by the other tenants on the floor. And, the bathtub was in the kitchen, covered with a metal surface, which served as a counter near the sink! It was our corner in this land of plenty and it was just a

My husband and I with our first-born baby, Elaine in New York, 1947.

start. Lajbek, who became Leon, had to wait six months before he could join the musicians' union, and therefore was pedaling ties and socks in the factories, a very demeaning occupation for an accomplished musician. My heart ached for him.

On February 14 1947, Valentine's Day, our first baby, a beautiful girl, whom we named Elaine Ann, after both our mothers, was born. What a joy it was to hold this little human being that belonged to me in my arms. I loved being a mother! Motherhood was and is the most rewarding experience of my life. Oh, how I wished I had my mommy to guide me and show me the way.

Eighteen months later our second daughter arrived, a nine-pound girl, with dark hair and serious eyes, a beautiful child. We were a family. During my pregnancy with Alice Miriam, named after our fathers (initials only), Elaine clung to me constantly. I worried about so many things. I felt vulnerable. I talked myself into believing that since I never had a grandmother, and my children didn't have one, neither would my grandchildren have one. I feared that something would happen to me and the cycle would continue.

Our family of four: Leon, Elaine and our second baby daughter, Alice in New York, 1948.

> *But I was lucky again! Our five wonderful grandchildren, whom we adore, have a grandmother! Marci, Hayley, Wendy, Stephanie, and Marc, the happiness you bring us is beyond words! May you grow up in a world of peace and love.*

The Lower Eastside was lively. Every week new arrivals appeared and pretty soon we were a "fraternity" of refugees or "greenhorns" ready to begin new lives.

In the meantime, my husband started learning a new occupation, one that was completely foreign to him but one frequently offered to newly arrived refugees. My Uncle Murray had a friend who owned a lady's suit factory and was very willing to give Lajbek a chance. So he started sewing on a machine but was determined that this job would only be temporary, a means to an end. He returned home every morning disgusted and disenchanted with his new homeland and occupation. So he put together a little orchestra and got weekend jobs playing at weddings and parties of people who knew him from Europe. This helped make ends meet, but deep down he was also hoping that eventually this could be his livelihood. Realizing this was not something he could easily achieve, he perfected the craft of sewing, went to school nights and weekends to study pattern making and design, and decided to look for bigger things.

Life in New York was difficult for him; therefore, after seeing an ad in the *New York Post* that read, "Looking for a foreman willing to relocate to Pennsylvania . . ." he thought, "Willing? We were eager to relocate." He jumped at the opportunity.

Leon traveled to Pennsylvania, all dressed up in a professional suit, walked into the shop, and was told to sit down at the machine. What disappointment. He would be a working foreman. Not what he was hoping for, but it was a start. After a few weeks we packed our things and moved to Pennsylvania.

As soon as we arrived in this small northeastern town, an enormous feeling of loneliness overwhelmed me. I felt cut off from other survivors with whom we became friendly, with whom we already had a bond. In this small town we were the *only* survivors. We truly were "aliens."

The Jewish community, which consisted of ninety families, embraced us warmly and tried to make us feel at home. My husband had his job, however unsatisfactory, my girls attended school, but for me, there was nothing to do—nothing to uplift me, though I did frequent the only Movie Theater in town.

I attempted a job as a salesperson in a dress shop, but I was too honest. When ladies tried on dresses, I gave my opinion as to how they looked. I could not talk a customer into a purchase that I did not think was flattering. Needless to say, this sales strategy didn't sit well with the boss and I was fired.

Several weeks later my brother-in-law, Leon's brother Beno, joined us in Pennsylvania. With our sponsorship he had just arrived in the United States from Germany with his pregnant wife, Ruth, and daughter Elizabeth. They lived with us in our two-bedroom apartment and it felt good to be surrounded by family.

The local newspaper came to interview the new arrivals and wrote about the reunion of two brothers, separated by war. One survived concentration camps with the help of his violin; the other survived Siberia where being a doctor (as Beno was) was his advantage. Their father planned well for his sons; without realizing it, he equipped them with skills that kept them alive.

We were celebrities. When my nephew Mark was born, the whole Jewish community brought gifts for the newborn. People noticed us. We were different. I saw this period of time, when we were the focus of attention, as an opportunity to reach out and educate the community. This was where my mission began.

I started speaking with my neighbors and my community about the horrors of Auschwitz, Bergen-Belsen, the Death March, etc. Most of the people in this town had never met a survivor. Some had never even heard of the Holocaust.

Living in this small town also gave me the opportunity to become a Hebrew School teacher for the handful of Jewish children in the synagogue's school. The Temple had a Rabbi, but could not afford to hire a certified teacher.

How I welcomed this opportunity to convey the little knowledge I had to these wonderful children whose parents wanted them to have a Jewish education and be prepared for Bar Mitzvahs. And how grateful they were to have me teach their children. I became part of the community. I started sewing little dresses for my girls from fabric remnants I bought by the pound. My children took piano, singing and dancing lessons. It paid off! When the Temple held a child talent show, my two little girls played a piano duet, sang "Sisters," and won first prize! What pride I felt!

Elaine and Alice have continued to perform "Sisters" all these years, even to the present, changing the words to suit the occasion. We never tire of it.

After four years we outgrew the small town we lived in. We needed more opportunities for the children and my husband had already acquired a better job with a bigger company that offered potential for continued advancement. So, we moved again, and this time stayed for twenty years.

Chapter 28

THE GOOD LIFE

Life was good. The children were growing. The city we moved to was also in northeastern Pennsylvania with a large, active Jewish community and quite a few survivor families. My husband eventually went to work for a large dress company and worked his way up to Vice-President. Success! Only in America!

Throughout the years, my husband has played with symphony orchestras and has performed concerts pro bono. He was happy to have music in his life and we were so proud of him.

I joined a group of wonderful ladies who played Mah Jongg practically every day. We enjoyed each other's company, took trips to New York to see Broadway shows, and frequented fine restaurants. We all had a marvelous time and have remained friends to this day.

I also became a certified. Hebrew teacher, a career that began shortly after moving to Pennsylvania and which lasted twenty-five years. Again my good education (though cut short) provided by my parents, gave me the foundation and tools that enabled me to do something meaningful.

I loved teaching and ever so gently told my students, my children and grandchildren about the Holocaust. After all, they did see my number and inquired about it. Years later, my three-year-old granddaughter asked me,

"Nanny, what is that number on your arm?"

"It's my telephone number, dear Marci. It's on my arm so I'll remember it," I replied.

Of course as she got older, she, as well as my other grandchildren, were told the truth by their mothers and me. My grandchildren have taken courses in Holocaust Studies, read extensively, and have written papers on this subject throughout their school and college years. My grandson Marc, eight years old at the time, wrote an essay in school about his "Grandmother with the number on her arm." My grandchildren are truly my legacy!

When my husband retired we moved to Florida, where I also enjoyed a twenty-year career as an interior decorator. I was not in any way trained for it but possessed a natural flair and loved working with people. It was a most rewarding way in which to express my creativity. I learned to play bridge and poker and loved both. Life was good.

I continued to be active in Holocaust education and frequently spoke at schools and community events. I initiated an annual gathering of survivors from Zaglembie, the region in Poland of which Bendzin was a part. The Zaglembie Gathering continues to this day under the leadership of all the people who were part of it during my years in Florida.

Eventually, my husband and I moved back north to be near our dear family, which became our top priority. Our wandering has come to an end. The good life continues. I still play bridge and Mah Jongg, continue my involvement in Holocaust education, and enjoy reading, seeing shows and watching movies.

We enjoy life to the fullest surrounded by our children and grandchildren who shower us with love and affection. We never end a phone conversation without saying, "I love you".

We are a very close-knit family and feel very blessed!

What a nice ending for a little girl from Poland with a little talent and a lot of luck!

Rose at a Zaglembie gathering with Benjamin Mead, the Keynote speaker, 1990.

Rose and other survivors at the first survivors' gathering in Israel, 1981. They are displaying their numbers that were tattooed on their left arms, in Auschwitz. Rose's number is 50887.

Picture taken during one of the annual Zaglembie gatherings. Everyone pictured here attended Gimnazium with Rose.

Rose addressing a class of future interviewers of Holocaust Survivors at the Documentation Center in Miami.

Rose, in 1993, speaking at Friends of Disabled War Veterans (She was secretary of the chapter)

Rose addressing the Zaglembie group in Miami Beach.

My daughters Elaine (right) and Alice (left) with me at the World Gathering of Holocaust Survivors in Washington, 1983.

EPILOGUE

My story began more than sixty years ago. It is for my two children and five grandchildren that I finally undertook the task of writing about it. I am so fortunate to remember all of the events in my life though the memories are very painful. Time heals wounds, but our wounds are too deep to be healed. Perhaps they are pushed deeper into our psyche, but they are never healed.

We were distracted by life itself—coming to and adopting a new country, a new language, giving birth, and raising two wonderful daughters who blessed us with five grandchildren, all of whom are aware of their heritage and connection to the Holocaust. I wanted them to know where they came from. It is for them and because of them that I have been involved in Holocaust education practically since liberation, before the subject was popular. And, weren't my mother's last words,

"Róziu, try to survive and tell the world"?

In 1946, when we came to the United States nobody spoke about the Holocaust. The survivors were eager to start new lives and talking was still too painful.

Historians had not yet begun their task of recording this dark period in the annals of history. But the number on my left arm provoked stares and questions. At first, I said it was my social security number or my telephone number, but eventually I decided that it was high time to educate those interested enough to ask questions. People asked me in line at the supermarket, at the gas station, in the park. That was in the early 1950's. As time went on the questions were more like:

"Is this what I think it is?"

"Yes, it is," I replied, and offered to answer anything they wanted to know, usually choking on tears. But I felt good about it. Isn't this why I had survived—to speak for those who hadn't.

And every time our family gathers around the holiday table, I look around me and think, "Hitler did not succeed, and I am so lucky!"

Being close in proximity to my family makes this the happiest time of my life. I still cry at the drop of a hat, but I am no longer as depressed or lonely. It sometimes feels as if I'm a child again, nurtured and protected by my family. We enjoy spending a lot of happy occasions together and we are equally there for each other during the inevitable stressful times in life.

Despite the guilt I often feel about being the only member of my family to survive, I am very grateful for

Rose and Leon in Florida, 1998

the privilege. I have lived a good and reasonably long life and I am happy for having written my story.

When my time comes to leave this earth, I know that my spirit will meet with those of my parents, siblings, and the rest of my martyred family. And together we will watch over our loved ones here on earth.

I will leave this world a happy woman!

My family on the occasion of our 50th Wedding Anniversary Party hosted by our children and grandchildren, August 5, 1995 in Atlantic City.

My family on the occasion of my 75th birthday with new additions to our family in 2001.

My daughters with me at my 75th Birthday party.

Rose's Poetry

The Joy of Motherhood
(1955)

How can I tell
What I feel in my heart,
The joy that I felt
Right from the start.

When I held in my arms
My baby girl or boy.
A greater love
I felt for no other.

For to have a child
Is such a joy
So thank you, G-d
For making me a mother.

Rose Ickowicz Rechnic

How Time Flies
(1975)

Where are my little babes so sweet,
Who used to love my touch?
Where are those little tapping feet?
I miss them so much.

Where are the days
When with a kiss I used to dry their tears?
Oh how I miss
Those dear old bygone years.

When Mommy's words were not absurd
But meant she's to show the way
Not like today you hear them say,
"That was in the olden days."

Where are my little girls so sweet
I'm wondering somehow
And as I look around I see
My little babes are big girls now.

Life's Mystery
(1978)

Life is so beautiful
And yet full of sorrow,
Filled with anxiety
About the vast tomorrow.

What will it bring?
What's for us in store?
Is there pain ahead?
Will we suffer more?

Or rejoice instead ... how I wish
I could see the future bright,
Not worry or brood.
What will be or might.

And enjoy today,
There's so much to do,
To be happy and gay
And leave the rest to YOU.

Soliloquy on my 60th Birthday
(1985)

Today is my 60th birthday
It's an eternity! Sixty years of joy and happiness,
Pain and suffering ...Where have they gone?
It only seems like yesterday—I was a child
In my hometown, surrounded by loving family,
Pampered by uncles, aunts, grandparents.
The memories of that former life, so vivid in my
mind . . .

And then the war! Death and suffering,
My constant companions. I lost father, brother
Then sister, mother.
Oh, how I miss them all!
Then liberation and rebirth—
From childhood to maturity
Youth lost forever.

A void throughout my life
Young years wasted in camps
From childhood
To married woman and motherhood.
A child myself I cried out for <u>my</u> mother

continued next page ...

Soliloquy continued

When myself I became one.
Loving to care for my little ones
Hugging them, holding them ...
But how often I needed my mom
To hug, to comfort, to guide me.
I wanted my children to be spared any suffering.
I have suffered enough but would have
Gladly suffered more to alleviate theirs.
I brought them into this world and I
Want so much for them to be happy.
I pray to my martyred family above:
May your sacred souls
Watch over your grandchildren and their children,
So they may carry our legacy
And grow up safe and happy
Among all the children of Israel.
Happy Birthday to me!

Hope
(1990)

When you have been on the brink of death
Do you ask yourself how good it is

To be alive, to have another chance . . .
I hope your answer is yes.

It's great to see the people you love,
The flowers that grow, the sun that shines . . .

And don't you thank
The Almighty above?

I hope you find it in your heart
To forgive and forget, to accept people's flaws

We all have faults,
So let us have a brand new start.

Life is too short and so full of sorrow
But times of happiness too.

Let's go for it, it's there for us to grasp
And let's start a new tomorrow.

Appendix 1

Student Responses to Rose's Story

"I was very impressed by Rose's speech. I feel as if I am taking part in history by having the opportunity to hear survivors' testimonies. Seeing her number tattoo had a big effect on me. This made her story so real. . . that she never had it removed because she can never remove her memories. I can totally understand . . . It is almost as if the tattoo is a validation of her hurt and agony. She should be proud to be a survivor and I think she is . . ."

"Rose presents the human side of the Holocaust for she is what we must learn more about. I truly believe Rose was saved by a miracle and we all should think long and hard about her survival. She is but a flower that has come back to life and grows to show the world her beauty . . ."

"We met a survivor today. She was great. She brought tears to my eyes. Her tattoo made the story seem more real. Her story was touching and one that I shall never forget. The tears, which she cried for her lost ones, will never be forgotten. I put myself in her shoes and tried to imagine losing my loved ones. I swear my heart almost stopped that very second. Rose is an amazing woman who continues to show great courage for herself as well as her long lost family. . ."

"Yet again I am blown away. In class we had a speaker who "escaped from Auschwitz." Sounds like a movie title . . . she was awesome! She took me in with her story . . . she had my full attention. Her story was one of the most unbelievable that I have ever heard. This strong minded, strong willed, "STRONG WOMAN" has endured so much. We feel our lives are so hard, but they are nothing compared to these survivors. The nightmares that they endure . . . must be mind boggling. I had a dream about it, and I am just a man who listened to her story. If I could be affected by just listening to her story, I cannot even imagine what a night of sleep must be like for her . . ."

"I think the entire class witnessed one of the most courageous acts of the human spirit today. Rose Rechnic, a survivor of Auschwitz and an escapee, told us her story. I was riveted . . . as I traveled back with her on her journey through the Holocaust. Her suffering, loss, and despair were felt in every fiber of my body, and I am haunted with each new revelation of bestiality. And yet here stands a woman of courage, fortitude, and hope for our future, sharing painful memories that bring tears to all our eyes. She, in moments of despondence, wishes she had the courage to take her life. I believe she had the greater courage to live and fulfill a very special task—to "enlighten" future generations to the importance of tolerance. I have been forever transformed . . ."

Appendix 2

GLOSSARY OF TERMS

Appell; Zählappell—Roll call in the concentration camps.

Aufschtehen; wstawadz—Get up.

Austeigen—Get out.

Boisko—A large field where sports activities took place.

Blockälteste; blockelder—Head of a barrack.

Cretze—Scabs resulting from scratching your body.

Death March—The march that concentration camp prisoners were forced to go on following the dissolution of concentration camps.

Diaspora—The scattering of Jews throughout the world who live outside of the homeland of Israel.

Durchfall—Dysentery; illness following typhoid.

Entlausung—Disinfecting for lice.

Entlausung Kammer—Area used for delousing.

Ferfluchte Juden—Parszywe Zydy—Derogatory insult directed at Jews, meaning "contaminated Jew."

Folksdeutche—Gentiles of German descent.

Ghetto—Enclosed area from which the Jews were prohibited from leaving.

Geiger—Violin player.

HIAS—Hebrew Immigrant Aid Society. Jewish organization that assists immigrants in resettling.

Judenrein—Free of Jews.

Judenrat—A Jewish government within the German government, formed within the ghetto.

Kaddish—Hebrew mourner's prayer for the dead.

Kapo—Head of work detail in camps.

Kehila—A committee of Jewish elders who helped the poor and afflicted.

Kencarte—A certificate for food rations and proof of employment.

Kirschnerei—A shop where furs were worked on.

Kommando Canada—Division of prisoners who assorted clothing of newly arrived transports.

Koya—Wooden bunks on which concentration camp prisoners slept.

Lager—Camp

Mach schnell—Make it fast.

Mein Kampf—The book written by Adolf Hitler (published in the early 1930's), which outlined his plan to annihilate the Jewish race.

Mussellman—Camp description of an emaciated person.

Nehstube—Where prisoners repaired German uniforms.

Judenrat—A Jewish government within the German government, formed within The Ghetto.

Ouserkommandos—Work outside of camp perimeter.

Pajdka—Chunk (of bread).

Revier—Concentration camp infirmary.

Schreiberin—person in charge of roll call (Appell/Zählappell).

Selection—Event singling out prisoners for extermination.

Sonderkommando—Prisoners whose job it was to remove gassed bodies and put them in ovens for cremation.

Sztubowas—Prisoners in charge of cleaning the barracks.

Unionwerke—Ammunition factory.

Washkiche—Laundry.

Zwangsarbeitslager—Forced labor camp.